REINCARNATION:
THE VIEW FROM ETERNITY

by

O. T. Bonnett, M.D.

In Collaboration with

Gregor Alan Satre

For permission, or serialization, condensation, adaptions, or for catalog of other publications, write to: Ozark Mountain publishing, Inc., P.O. Box 754, Huntsville, AR 72740, Attn: Permissions Department.

Library of Congress Cataloging-in-Publication Data
Bonnett, O.T. - 1925 -
Satre, Gregor Alan - 1943 -
"Reincarnation: The View from Eternity" by O.T. Bonnett and Greg Satre
A medical doctor of 44 years explores the nature of reincarnation and man's role in the universe.
1. Metaphysics   2. Reincarnation   3. Philosophy
I. Bonnett, O.T., 1925 -   II. Satre, Gregor A., 1943 -   III. Title

Library of Congress Catalog Card Number: 2005929065
ISBN: 1-886940-88-6

Cover Art and Layout by www.enki3d.com
Book Design: Julia Degan
Book Set in: Times New Roman

www.ozarkmt.com
Printed in the United States of America

Dedicated to

My guide and eternal companion
Pan

With special thanks to the late

Dr. Ralph Warner

Anyone interested in having the author conduct seminars or
give lectures on metaphysics or self-healing,
please contact:

O.T. Bonnett, M.D.
P.O. Box 1272
Raton, NM 87740

Telephone: (505) 445-2847
E-mail: BONNETT12345@MSN.COM

Other books by O.T. Bonnett:

Confessions of a Healer
Why Healing Happens

Table of Contents

Preface

This book presents a metaphysical discussion of the nature of the Universe and mankind's relationship to it. Metaphysics is a philosophical approach to understanding the Universe as a sentient being, lending richness and greater awareness to our lives. Over time, thoughts and beliefs concerning the Universe, evolution, multiple incarnations, and the nature of mankind have been distorted by various individuals and institutions, leaving many of us confused. Indeed, we often hold beliefs that are totally at odds with the true character of things. For this reason, it will be necessary to occasionally examine various concepts in which these other doctrines have created turmoil and misunderstanding.

This is a collaborative work. It represents a blending of ideas, thoughts, and experiences of myself and those of Gregor Alan Satre who collaborated with me in this task. It is an accounting of what we learned during our personal journeys in the exploration of consciousness. These journeys were accomplished both separately and in concert. Without our combined effort, this work would not exist in its present form. Over the past sixteen years or so, Greg and I spent many days together, discussing metaphysics into the wee hours of the morning, but most often, we talked on the telephone – hours on end. Together, we worked and struggled to express our thoughts and to relate our experiences in simple, understandable language. It has not been easy. We are well aware that some of the ideas will be totally new to the reader and not based upon anything that has ever before been expressed – at least as far as we know. Much of the specific metaphysical information presented is knowledge gained as the result of a "white light" event that Greg experienced more than thirty years ago. During this lengthy experience, he was taken out-of-body by two of his former teachers, Chien Tre-csi and Cheng Lo, and shown the Universe in all its splendor – its interacting fields of conscious, intelligent energy. The event was so awesome that it was a good two years before he could utter a single coherent sentence to express what he had seen and learned.

We were laughing together one day when it occurred to us that we were in a very enviable position, free to express our ideas without fear of reprisal. I am a retired physician, an author, and a sculptor. Greg is a potter and a psychic of unbelievable abilities. He is working on books of his own. Neither of us belongs to any organization that will be offended by our philosophical stance or that has any power over us. Greg and I spend a lot of time just laughing together. While the rest of the world goes about like Buddhists, frowning over the bitterness and the suffering of life, or like Confucianists with a sour expression because life is not going according to their plan, Greg and I have been laughing our way along like a couple of old Tao masters, enjoying the harmony and disharmony afforded by the trials and adventures that life has offered.

We are living in an age of specialization. We see evidence of this all about. At the same time, the explosion of technical information has overwhelmed us to the point that many find it impossible to keep up with the changes taking place within their own field of endeavor. To a degree, having so much knowledge at hand is helpful, providing it does not confuse us, but it is also a deterrent to having a broad view of what is going on in the world about.

In this culture, we are trained to compartmentalize our knowledge by teachers who focus their attention on narrower and narrower aspects of their subject. I know of no educational institution where students are given a broad, integrated view of the subjects they are studying. This was certainly true when I went to medical school, and I seriously doubt that much change has taken place. The result of this narrow perspective amounts to what can be considered a cognitive defect in our ability to perceive a vaster Truth. This educational aberration confronts individuals who spend entire lifetimes studying a single, specific thing and mastering the appropriate jargon, only to find themselves incapable of communicating with specialists in other fields, to say nothing of artists, philosophers, theologians, and ordinary people.

For this reason, the subject material of this book will not be limited to a singular view of the Universe. It is a philosophical discussion of the physics of reality, multiple incarnations, and metaphysical esoterica. I give reasons for man's existence in multiple incarnations, speak in general of the philosophy of metaphysics, quantum mechanics, and the theory of relativity. In addition, I address, among other topics, matter and energy, non-local connections within matter, how the psyche creates the physical world, and give new insights concerning the theory of evolution.

Philosophy is not separate from physics, nor are physics and quantum mechanics separate from life. Indeed, the concepts involved in understanding these subjects are the same and in many ways even expressed using the same words and phrases. The Universe is a continuum of intelligent consciousness, and we are inseparable from it. The only boundaries are artificial, placed there by people who fail to grasp the wholeness of it all. For any person to continue living, bound by a focused, narrow belief system, is a tragedy of great proportion.

Some of the concepts presented will appear strange and hard to accept by the reader – at least at first. But the ideas are not difficult to comprehend for I have struggled to keep the language as simple as possible. Nowhere in the book have I used "insider" terms that only those initiated into some private cult of thinking will understand. On the other hand, the subjects I discuss are not "fluff" nor are they like a romance novel that can be skimmed over in an evening "just to catch the gist."

The concepts are not presented in a shallow, glib manner as we are so accustomed to in this day and age. Neither are they presented as speculations to ruminate about and never act upon. Perhaps, more than at any other time in history, we demand quick, easy solutions to life – the five second sound byte or video clip, the condensed novel, the one paragraph summary at the beginning of an article, midnight basketball, and other quick fixes to profound and troubling issues that face our culture. I believe it is time to put this superficial take on life aside. It is time to exercise our intellectual muscles for a change and take responsibility for our lives. In one respect, the destruction of the World Trade Center and the associated disasters call us to do just that.

My personal guide, Pan, has been my companion and mentor from the "beginning of time". Like a good Zen master, sometimes He has knocked me to my knees during moments of triumph, forcing me to reassess my position and keep the Wheel of Self-realization turning. He skillfully guided my inquiries with insights and lessons and was largely responsible for my meeting many persons who have been of great help. Pan directly furnished me with critical information which has been included in the manuscript. He informs me that the content of this book contains no misinformation given the built-in difficulties associated with communicating concepts and ideas that are actually beyond words, not to mention the difficulty of getting past the limits of my finite knowledge and comprehension of the Universe. Pan's affirmation of approval means a great deal to me whether it means anything at all to the reader. On the other hand, I am well aware that this book, like any other on metaphysics, is incomplete. There is always more to learn as one's apperceiving basis expands with knowledge, experience, and time.

In 1961, I met Karlfried Graf von Durkheim, a physician and an author, while attending a medical conference in Italy. In one of our lengthy conversations, he explained the Zen Wheel of Self-realization to me. He said there were five spokes – five steps to self-awareness:

> The first is to acquire critical awareness whereby you realize what is missing from your life and what is wrong.
> The second involves letting go of all that anchors and holds you in your present state.
> The third requires unification with your essential being, liberating you from the grip of your ego.

The fourth is acceptance of the call of that inner vision and the beginning of your new responsibility.

The fifth and last is the attempt to put your new vision into action and, of course, you fail. But thanks to your critical awareness whereby you realize what is missing from your life and what is wrong ... so turns the wheel.

So it will be with many who read this book, but after you have had a chance to assimilate the information contained herein, you should have a more complete grasp of the cosmos and of yourself. It is only through knowledge that humankind can assume control of its destiny and cease to wander aimlessly, and sometimes with malice, through life. Adopting a philosophy which includes a metaphysical approach to the Universe will enable us to rise up, becoming the benevolent and loving seekers of wisdom that we are intended to be. We must keep in mind that the entire purpose of individuated human consciousness is to attain wisdom. To the degree that goal is achieved, each of us can contribute to the wisdom of the Universe.

Introduction
The Beginning

I was asleep but aware that I was about to have the "special dream" again. As always, it started with a heavy pressure over my left cheek bone as if someone was pushing very hard with their thumb. Then I was falling face down with my arms and legs spread outward. As I fell, it seemed as if I was rotating about that point of pressure in my face. Slowly, I spiraled down, down, down into blackness. There was a hint of nausea, but not enough to be unpleasant. This time, I was determined to hold on to the feeling I was about to experience. Deeper and deeper I sank until I reached the bottom, but there was no impact. I just stopped. There was a loud noise like a snap, and I was surrounded by blackness. The sensation was awesome, as if I was suspended in deep space. I was not aware of a body. It seemed as if I was nothing but pure consciousness and anything I wanted to know was available to me. It was wonderful! The dream was one of the most exhilarating experiences I have ever had. I tried to hold on to the sensation, but it vanished as always like a bursting bubble. Then the dream within the dream was gone, and I became aware that I was in my bed at the level where I started, sleeping comfortably.

Sometimes it would begin all over, and again, I would resolve to retain that feeling of pure consciousness – but I never could. It only lasted a few moments. As a tiny infant and a small child, I experienced the dream three or four times a week. As I grew older, it occurred with less frequency. It has been about sixty years since I had the dream, but I remember it with great clarity.

I was deeply hypnotized, lying on the floor in my living room. My friend, Jeff, had hypnotized me. Once I attained the trance, I immediately brought back the memory of a life in about

1850. I saw myself running straight toward the army lieutenant; my big hunting knife clutched in my hand; my long hair secured with a wide cloth headband; I could hear my scream and the "pat pat" of my moccasins pounding on the earth. I was determined to kill until I was killed. The others were fools to accept life on a reservation. I could not comprehend why they would agree to something so totally unjust and give up all our land in exchange for a little piece of worthless desert of rocks and sand. There was little game or water. I had done all I knew to keep the intruders out. I killed every white man I could, stealing into camps at night and killing all but one, leaving him to awaken in the morning to find his companions with their throats cut and their bowels spilled on their blankets and the sand. The survivor, hopefully, would hurry back to wherever he had come from and warn others to keep away. I had a clear recollection of the feeling of hot blood as it sprayed and gushed over my hand as my knife cut open their throats.

I was sick of killing; I did not enjoy it; my tactic of terror had failed; the whites kept coming; I would not go to the hated reservation; it was time to die. I watched them set the ambush for me. I knew where every soldier was hidden. I ran into the little clearing among the rocks and almost got to him when the lieutenant stood, raised his pistol, and shot me point blank in the face. The bullet struck me in the left cheek and entered my brain. My spirit watched as they rushed out of their hiding places, hooting and shouting for joy. They were confident they had fooled me with the trap, never suspecting that I could have killed most of them where they hid and escaped unseen as I had done before. They gathered about shooting and kicking my lifeless body. Several of them spat upon me. One enlisted man unbuttoned his pants and urinated in my face. Then they left my body in the blood, and urine, and sand, and rode off.

Jeff brought me out of my trance. I was excited. I had made the connection with my lifelong dream. The recurring dream had been that of my death as the Apache Indian shot down by the army lieutenant. What a marvelous adventure in learning. I realized that the ability to recall or at least be knowledgeable of other lives might be very helpful for most people.

In my books *Confessions of a Healer* and *Why Healing Happens*, I made a number of references to reincarnation. I realized at the time that I needed to deal with the subject from a different perspective and from a deeper level than that of most books on the topic. I also understood that to do justice to the subject it would require, at the very least, an entire book. I believe, if one understands the Universe, the true nature of man, and his interrelationship with the Universe, then accepting the concept of multiple incarnations is not difficult nor the idea strange.

Coming to accept the validity of multiple incarnations was a major factor in understanding my proper role as a physician. Prior to gaining this insight, I agonized with the families of my patients when they died, leaving their loved ones. Often death seemed premature. Children died with no chance at life. One patient saved his money all his life with the expectation of buying a motor home and touring the country upon his retirement only to have a massive stroke the day after he retired. People seemed trapped in a morass of pain and circumstances that appeared to be none of their making. Where was the justice we were supposed to find in life when decent, good people had terrible things happen?

Accepting the truth of multiple incarnations allowed many things to fall into place and offered a view of medical practice from a new, exciting, and a much more mature perspective. This new stance made sense and brought justice into the picture of life. Accepting a totally new framework of belief is not easy, but it can be fun, and it is certainly rewarding. I have been caught up in the continuous process of restructuring my belief system as I acquired each new bit of information. It is a worthy task and, of course, has no end. My journey has been ongoing for over seventy-five years. However, it is one which I feel is critical for anyone seriously interested in being a true human being. Understanding his nature is one of man's primary goals. Indeed, only by appreciating the view within can we fulfill our creative potential.

The hard task, I knew, would be to present the ideas and concepts so they would be readily understood by the average reader. On the other hand, I did not wish to address the subject in an oversimplified manner that would appear childish and be rejected out of hand by the more knowledgeable individual. Eric Hoffer, a philosopher of the 1950s, declared that communication of ideas is dependent upon using terms and words with which the individual to whom you are talking is comfortable and familiar. He stated that there was no philosophical subject he could not discuss with his fellow dock workers, regardless of how profound the topic might be. What made this possible was Hoffer's ability to phrase the concepts in simple, common language. Too often people are put off by the first word with which they are unfamiliar and cease to listen further. To communicate successfully, one must use language that is generally understood by all.

In the early 1970s, I met Ralph Warner at an open house given by a physicist who had been on the original committee assigned by the government to investigate UFO landings. Ralph and I became fast friends. He was a psychologist and a psychic of unsurpassed ability. He and his spiritual guide, Hector, were of great help to me in the last years of my practice. Occasionally, I would call him for help in making a diagnosis when the nature of the problem was not apparent. He was invariably correct as laboratory and X-ray studies later confirmed. He also helped clarify the answers to metaphysical questions during a time when I was learning about the Universe. I was deeply saddened by his death in 1997.

I met Greg Satre for the first time in 1987 when we were both doing an art show in Denver. I had already set up my booth of sculptures when Greg came puffing in, a bit late, and proceeded to set up his exhibit of pottery next to me. As I watched him, hovering over his pottery, I sensed something unusual about the man. From the way he handled the vases, pots, and other pieces, it was obvious that they meant more to him than what they appeared to be on the surface. They were more than pleasing shapes of fired and glazed clay. He handled and touched them as if they were his children. Then I looked at the pottery itself. It fairly spoke to me. The pieces were alive, each with a bit of his spirit inside. As Greg and I began to visit, it was as though we were continuing a conversation that had started long before. Customers were few, and we had hours each day to talk of things metaphysical. We have been friends ever since. Occasionally, we go to each other's house for a few days' visit. Our spirited conversations carry on into the wee hours of the morning like a couple of kids at camp with no counselor to tell us to turn off the lights and go to sleep.

Much of what I will present was formulated and modified during many hours of discussion between us. On numerous occasions, he or I would bring up some thought, and then, much to our delight, we would both dream about it the next night or two. Even when we were not visiting directly or talking on the telephone, it was obvious that at some psychic level we were in constant communication. Together, we worked out what appears to us the most logical way of presenting the knowledge we wish to impart. Jointly, we refined our ideas and concepts, using both his and my intuitive information gathered separately and in concert. Working together is not a new adventure for us. We have experienced two other significant incarnations together, but perhaps more important, we have known each other and worked together for eons in spiritual planes of existence.

From the time he was a child of three, Greg was physically and mentally tortured by his stepfather and his mother who orchestrated the abuse and participated as well. This went on daily for fifteen years. The details are unimportant but, because Greg never thought of himself as a victim, the ordeal stimulated him to learn and to develop uncommon psychic abilities. Greg experimented with out-of-body travel, practicing until he could get out of his body at will. He learned to "tune into" the energy patterns of trees and animals and communicate with them by means of thought pictures. He learned to develop a heat-shield so that he would not be harmed or feel pain when he was forced to hold burning matches and embers from the fire in his bare hands. He became a true seer – able to perceive objects, people, ideas, and thoughts as energy patterns and observe the interchange of energy about him.

When Greg was thirty-two, he had what he terms a "white light" experience that lasted nearly three hours by his clock. During this lengthy event, he was psychically taken to a "place" by two of his spirit guides and shown the Universe with all its energy forms, multiple realities, and layers of consciousness, relating and interacting one with the others. He has spent the ensuing years translating this experience into understandable language. He had similar events of shorter duration which were related to specific metaphysical questions. To date, he has been able to describe in words only about twenty percent of all he was shown – and knows. Understandably, the knowledge gained in these revealing experiences became the gold standard by which he judges all his other psychic experiences and the information he has acquired. The material presented here passed the gold standard, as well.

In general, my metaphysical insights have not come as dramatically or as suddenly. Much of my metaphysical knowledge has been a part of my thinking from my earliest childhood memories. Other insights have been presented to me over my lifetime, usually in subtle ways and not in the dramatic fashion that revelations seem to come to others. All my life I yearned to have psychic visions such as others experienced. Most of the time, when I found out what they learned through their mystical and meditational episodes, I was a bit let down and disappointed, for their revelations were things I had always known. I thought everyone else knew them, too, and the information was common knowledge. Through my friendship with Greg Satre and Ralph Warncr I came to realize that I possess a large amount of metaphysical information intuitively.

When I began to read metaphysics over sixty years ago, most of it seemed neither new or strange. I had one brief "white light" event in which I was shown the mechanism by which cells become cancerous and how to prevent it.[1] As I became involved writing this book, a lot of metaphysical information was given to me in a very direct manner. It came in the form of intuitive flashes and dreams on a more or less need to know basis. I credit my guide, Pan, for many of these revelations. Other insights, I am sure, are the result of psychic interchanges of information with Greg and Ralph and with entities of whom I have no direct knowledge.

My formal education was that of a doctor of medicine, an old medical dinosaur of sorts, a general practitioner, no less. As is true with almost all doctors, my training was funneled down a very narrow path of intense scientific study that left literally no time available to obtain a true education. In my search to find ways to help my patients when conventional methods failed, or so often proved to be of little value, I was led to unconventional forms of treatment and sometimes to the metaphysical or mystic aspects of reality which I then applied to my life and my practice. Using hypnosis, for example, I discovered that people could produce burns complete with blisters when they only thought they had been burned, and stop bleeding by simply willing it so. If, through suggestion, the mind could produce a burn or stop bleeding, I understood it could produce a disease and heal it as well. People could recall other incarnations with ease providing they were deeply hypnotized. Numerous things I observed did not have any traditional scientific explanation. If I was not to cast aside and ignore these observations, I had to fit them into a new idea construct, a new belief system that would allow both traditional and metaphysical explanations to exist in harmony.

Several years ago at an art show, I met a young woman who is a physician, specializing in joint diseases. We got to talking about the medical profession. To see how she would react, and to learn if she was truly interested in becoming a healer, I told her of some of the nontraditional activities with which I had been involved. She listened with a bewildered look on her face and

---

[1]Confessions of a Healer: MacMurray and Beck, Denver 1994

then said, "B...but you didn't follow any consistent plan of treatment. You had no direction in your professional life!" I looked at this nice, very rigid lady and replied, "Oh, yes, I was absolutely directed and totally consistent. I had one very clear goal which I pursued throughout my entire professional life. I actively sought wisdom." She did not reply, but walked away with her mouth actually hanging open.

Organization and division of the subject material presented in this book is arbitrary and artificial. When one is writing about a multilayered, dynamic, ever-changing, sentient Being, any division is artificial. Any description, by its very nature, introduces the possibility of error and misunderstanding. In writing this book, I have attempted to speak of the unspeakable. As a Tao master would say, "If you are able to speak of Tao, then it is not Tao of which you speak." Or in the words that novelist Herman Hesse attributes to the Buddha, "One can impart knowledge but not wisdom." In *Siddhartha*, Hesse has Buddha go on to explain that the wisdom the wise man tries to communicate to others always ends up sounding a bit foolish.

This book is an accounting of what Greg Satre and I learned through our experiences as we explored consciousness. It is a book of metaphysics and the ideas presented should be accepted for what they are − metaphysical concepts that embrace the Universe and humankind. While I was writing the first draft of this manuscript I was asked by what authority I took it upon myself to write about such subjects as physics, matter, and energy. The individual who asked was very sincere and quite put off by what she perceived to be an affront to the physicists and mathematicians who had spent their lives investigating the very topics I was discussing so freely. I replied that I was writing a book of philosophy and as such did not have to prove my statements by any scientific means other than the consistency of reason itself. I was, nonetheless, troubled by the charge and discussed it with Greg. He reminded me that the entire purpose of individuated human consciousness is to take part in the creative act. Because of the insights gained during this and other lives, we have been given the authority and opportunity to be part of the creative process. As I wrote, it occurred to me that throughout the forty-four years I practiced medicine, some nonphysician was forever telling me how I should practice my profession. Sometimes they were right. Now it is time to return the favor to another discipline.

Obviously, the new ideas and concepts contained in this book are totally unproven by any empirical, scientific method. I do not even have the means to document such proof should it exist. But the fact that I am unable to prove the statements I make should not, in itself, detract from their validity. Mathematicians and physicists are still trying to prove equations and concepts put forth by Einstein and others almost ninety years ago, and the equations are generally assumed to be valid.

Mankind lives in a spiritual world, a world of feelings, emotions, and sensations that has nothing to do with science. He may work and earn his living in a world of science and technology, but he lives in a spiritual one. Moreover, the things men live by are rarely provable in any absolute sense, nor are they provable by science. We do not demand proof. For example, prove by any scientific method that a sunset or a rose is beautiful. Prove to someone that you like butterscotch ice cream. By choosing that flavor frequently, you may only be punishing yourself for some imagined childhood guilt. How can you prove that you love your parents, or spouse, or children? Just because you may not abuse them is no proof. You do not abuse the stranger you meet in the grocery store, but I seriously doubt that you would claim to love her – at least not in the same way you love your family. None of the things you do or say can validate your love in any scientific or provable fashion.

In the spiritual realm, human feelings are generally accepted without question. Statements concerning passions are rarely challenged. If you say you hate someone or like another, people usually believe you. You are not questioned in the same manner as should you say that the Universe is a living being. Usually, we live and make decisions based upon emotions and feelings.

Scientists are wrong when they insist that, to be valid, the observations and experiences of men must be proven by established, scientific methods.

I will leave the job of documenting the truth of these ideas concerning the Universe and mankind to someone else, assuming they feel them worth the effort. In a sense, I have adopted the role much like that of a professor of theoretical mathematics or physics. I have put forth a number of new concepts which I believe are true. Let the world discuss them and determine whether I am correct or not. I have a strong hunch that if scientists attempt to validate the concepts advanced in this book a different language will be needed. Through the use of mathematics alone it will be difficult to address the idea that matter is conscious. How are spiritual things to be quantified? How can we prove they even exist? How much fear does a plant emote when it is threatened by fire? A few inches? How about a quart? You profess to love your spouse. Is your love measured in yards, pounds, or volts? The language to address these spiritual values is there. We do not even have to invent it. It is called philosophy. Scientists simply have to master a new vocabulary and learn to think in different terms.

In reading this book (or any other for that matter) keep in mind that all definitions, indeed, all words are metaphors. Every definition is nothing other than a symbol consisting of words which are themselves symbols, representing ideas or concepts. As such, no definition is capable of encompassing the entire meaning of an idea or concept. No metaphor is complete. We use them simply because language is inadequate and incomplete – and mankind is no longer consciously telepathic as he was in so-called primitive times or as he is now, during infancy.

In the process of thinking about new concepts, it is wise not to accept or reject them initially. One need not take a position saying, for instance, that the idea of multiple incarnations is poppycock and nothing will convince him otherwise. Taking a position on an issue without examining it first is not unlike standing on a teeter-totter to get a better view. It matters little which end one chooses to stand upon, for regardless of the position, they will find them self only a few inches above the ground. But, by standing in the middle, the view is greatly improved. By refusing to adopt a stance at the outset, both sides of the issue can be evaluated without feeling the necessity to defend one position or the other. This is not the same as failing to make a decision. It is just a better way to examine new ideas.

Whether the ideas and concepts offered in this book are accepted is of no real importance, although I hope that you have not made a heavily defended, premature commitment to reality. If you have not, the new concepts should, if nothing else, stimulate thought, stimulate the urge to read and, most importantly, stimulate the desire to look within yourself and recognize and reacquaint yourself with your Essential Being. Doing so, you will be opened to the joy of living and the fun and the sheer excitement of the world within and without.

CHAPTER 1

The Universe – A Sentient Being

It was a hot midsummer day, and I was lying on the floor of my living room in a deep hypnotic trance. Gradually, I became aware of my physical appearance. I was ancient, in fact, I was about one hundred twenty years old. My thin, white beard reached almost to my waist. I was Chinese living in what is now South Korea. At that time, toward the final years of the Han Dynasty, it was part of China. Jeff Morris, who hypnotized me, was listening intently while I described myself.

"What are you doing?" he asked.

"I'm walking along a steep path outside a village. There are perhaps two dozen folks of all ages following me. I'm teaching them about life – about the Universe. I think some of them are ill and following along in hope that I will treat them. I'm a physician-philosopher of sorts."

The day was beautiful and very bright, yet a thin layer of clouds hung low in the sky and the mountains rose upward to disappear into them. The sun was about to break through the mist. Brilliant yellow flowers like big buttercups blanketed the hillside on either side of the path. Then, as I took in the beauty of the scene, I became aware that the flowers were singing! The rocks and trees were singing as well!

"Jeff, the Earth is alive! Every portion of the Universe is singing in praise for being alive. Each part has its own musical

1

pitch. The trees, and grass, and flowers have their own unique tones, and the rocks, and earth, and water have their's in a lower register. They are all different, but they're combining into one glorious chord of sound, like the world is singing 'hallelujah.'"

"What religion are you?" Jeff asked.

"The same as I am now and always have been. I follow Tao," my voice replied with confidence.

I went on to explain that Tao is not a religion in the usual sense of the word. It is a concept – an attitude toward life and the Universe. As I lay hypnotized, listening to the Earth singing, quite suddenly another thought came to me. God did not create the Universe! *God is the Universe.* The Universe and God are one-and-the-same. Wow, what a concept!

We discussed this and other revelations which were presented to me as I recalled this particular incarnation. Then I came out of hypnosis. The Universe is alive? God and the Universe are identical? I had not thought of them in those terms before. The experience set me to thinking about the nature of mankind and of the Universe. Fortunately, I had a lot of help in my quest for enlightenment. There is much information available in books. Then I have the good fortune to have a number of friends who are gifted with fantastic psychic abilities. As I learned, I organized and integrated my own thoughts and insights with those of my mentors.

I have come to the conclusion that acceptance of the reality of multiple incarnations and the implications sustained by that knowledge is critical to the salvation of the human race as we know it. Actually, to talk of an incarnation, to say nothing of multiple incarnations, isolated from its deeper meaning, is to present the concept as a self-serving exercise with no goal other than personal development. The process is much more involved with an ultimate purpose far beyond the growth of one individual. Indeed, for the goal of multiple incarnations to be limited to the growth and maturity of a single person is short sighted. At one level, that is the purpose, but the larger purpose is for the developing human entity to contribute to the wisdom and the overall development and creative ventures of the Universe.

While I continued to explore my "past" lives and those of others through the use of hypnosis, I continued to inquire into the nature of mankind and the Universe. The belief from which I was working was no different than that of others in my generation or of the next generation for that matter. The belief structures we were taught were cut and dried. It is important for you to have some understanding of this framework of assumption.

When I was a boy in the 1920s and 1930s, the thinking of Planck, Einstein, Bohr, and other intuitive geniuses in the field of subatomic physics had yet to make an impact upon the world in general. The reality in which I grew up was a world of rigid, unchanging, mathematical and scientific laws in which matter was composed of solid particles. The smallest of these were atoms, and they behaved in predictable ways.

God was a spiritual being standing outside the Universe – somewhere in heaven – creating the machinery, pulling the strings, and flipping the switches to keep it running. Mankind was also a creation, made in His image, placed on Earth and destined to follow the laws He laid down. Man's only purpose was to love, honor, and serve this God – a God of paradoxical actions and attitudes. He was considered to be a loving, forgiving, and benevolent father while, at the same time, a God of wrath and vengeance who destroyed whole nations for the benefit of a group who were the chosen ones.

The concept of a God separate from the world attained explicit structure and blessing primarily in Judeo-Christian thinking. Other world religions were wrestling with this problem of separation as well, but it was more clearly stated by Judaism. This idea of God apart from the Universe, or if you prefer, mind separate from matter, attained positive validation and blessing in the philosophy of Rene Descartes who expounded this concept in the mid 1600s. Most important of all, Descartes reached an agreement with the Church. According to the compromise, science excluded any involvement or discussion of spiritual matters from its domain, and the Church agreed to cease its persecution of the scientists should their discoveries vary from accepted religious dogma. Finally, Newton's mathematics made it possible to place these concepts into a formalized structure, resulting in a standardized approach to scientific inquiry. Descartes' philosophy and Newton's mathematics provided the tools for a major change to develop in nonreligious, Western thinking of the seventeenth century and launched the beginning of the Scientific Era.

Prior to this, in 1609, Galileo invented the telescope and was able to prove the idea, previously introduced by Copernicus in 1543, that the Earth was not the center of the Universe. Sadly, Copernicus and Galileo were a bit premature. They made their discoveries before Descartes's bargain was accomplished. Galileo essentially backed down from his stated scientific position after a long argument with the Church and was sentenced to a life of imprisonment in his villa rather than being excommunicated. About seventy years before, Copernicus remained fast in his belief and refused to say he was wrong. Among other things, he was punished by having his brilliant work "black listed."

Early on, investigators were concerned with the *meaning* of things and what *purpose* they might serve. They were concerned with understanding the *meaning behind* various phenomena. This was a carry-over from primitive times when humans understood that they contributed to the physical events that went on about them. For example, early human beings believed their emotions augmented the development of storms and natural disasters. As time went on, thoughts, beliefs, and physical events were closely associated. Floods were thought of as Nature's way of wiping the slate clean of human strife and starting over. Earthquakes were the result of human emotional unrest and upheaval being reflected by the Earth. However, after Descartes' philosophy was accepted, such spiritual connections were never again considered. He further postulated that only scientific knowledge was absolute and must be based entirely upon mathematics. After that, nothing was accepted as valid unless it could be expressed mathematically and incorporated into a formula or an equation and proved by the sciences of mathematics and statistics. This led to the conclusion that the Universe and its creatures were little more than machinery to be studied and tinkered with by means of mathematical equations. Thanks to Descartes, matter and mind, science and religion were forever separated. These were the principles of thought upon which Western science was founded.

Scientific inquiry became the only acceptable way to acquire knowledge. Any information obtained intuitively or conclusions based upon reason or personal experience were considered suspect, if not invalid. Philosophers were considered to be little more than impractical, unreliable, undisciplined dreamers and of no consequence. And this attitude exists today. A few years ago, a western university with which I am familiar disbanded its entire philosophy department that served several hundred students in order to fund the purchase of more computers for the science departments.

Bowing to the dictates of Descartes, scientific experiments were designed to remove any form of judgment or influence on the part of scientists from the situation. All experiments were designed in such a way as to reduce every element to some numerical value and the data recorded. Scientists were trained to make no interpretations whatsoever but to subject the data to statistical analysis in order to find out what had been learned. In earlier times, as men began to investigate the nature of things, physics and metaphysics were considered to be one subject. Scientists were also philosophers, but Descartes essentially put an end to that.

Mankind became obsessed with science, finding the mechanisms by which things worked and how they might be altered. Of what was matter composed? Every artificially produced particle of energy found in a bubble chamber was named and its discovery heralded as a great advance. What were the underlying mathematical formulae that would pull it all together? What was the germ or virus causing every illness? Now, we expect to find a gene to explain every disease, physical abnormality, and behavior. Indeed, over the centuries science became a god.

Prior to the scientific era man concerned himself with the meaning of events and what purpose certain actions served. Questions of this nature, addressing concepts of purpose and meaning, were not capable of being converted to mathematical terms. So, the questions ceased being asked. As we know, once Descartes successfully separated matter and mind, scientists were precluded from asking questions involving spiritual values, meaning, or purpose. That the scientific community took to this format without reservation is well documented. Perhaps the willingness of the scientists lay in the fact that the ultimate purpose of many scientific inquiries is counter to the best interests of mankind.

Most of the world was at odds with mechanically oriented Western thinking – not that this bothered the Westerners. Eastern thought did not view the world as a machine. Eastern philosophy visualized the Universe as a dynamic balance between spirit and matter, acting and reacting within greater areas of influence which were themselves in a dynamic balance. To Eastern thinkers, nothing was absolute for the Universe was always in a state of flux, a state of constant change. To the East, there was always an element of uncertainty.

Unfortunately, at least from the stand point of furthering philosophical development, the Western approach to science and technology gave rise to lots of things; "toys" which the world seemed to want. Western scientific investigation veered completely away from philosophical thought. At the same time, scientific discoveries led to the production of goods and thrived on competition in which individuals were valued only in terms of their potential to buy and produce more things. Even the East was attracted by the glitter of shiny, material products that it

6

seemed to desire. To some degree, the East lost its center, as well.

Being a white, middle class Westerner growing up in Kansas, Wyoming, and Illinois, I was completely unaware of anything beyond the Judeo-Christian teachings and a physical world based upon Cartesian-Newtonian concepts. To have a sudden, clear revelation that the Universe was a living, sentient Being and synonymous with God completely shattered every belief I held.

*** The Universe is intelligent consciousness actualized into physical reality by intent.***

The Universe is a sentient Being! It is a living Entity! Every part of the Universe is conscious, aware, precognitive, and has memory, intent, and the ability to communicate and create. These seven qualities of life pervade every single quantum making up every electron, proton and neutron. For this reason, in the very real sense of the word, every atom is alive regardless of its location or function in the Universe. It matters not whether it is an atom in a wisp of breeze, a raindrop, a tree, a butterfly, or a human being. Every atom possesses these qualities: consciousness, awareness, communication, memory, intent, creativity, and precognition. Even a rock is a living entity, exhibiting all these attributes at its own unique level of existence.

Since these traits are essential characteristics of matter, it is appropriate to discuss their meaning within the framework of an atom, for example. Consciousness means that the atom has the potential of knowing – knowing that it exists, what it is doing, and what is happening.

Awareness adds another dimension beyond consciousness. It means that, beyond the potential of knowing, the atom does know. It is consciously aware of its surroundings and knowledgeable of its present location and function within the molecule or structure of which it is a part. Thus, consciousness and awareness, though they are similar in meaning, have certain implied and obviously critical differences.

7

Communication and memory mean no more or less than the words imply. Atoms do, indeed, communicate with each other. They possess the ability to know where they are and remember where they have been. They can and do remember their function. But there is much more – they are precognitive. Recently, scientists have been puzzling over the results of an experiment that has shaken their mechanistic concept of the Universe. It is known that when light (photons) is directed at a reflective surface such as a wall and pass through a single hole in an opaque barrier, they produce a spot of light on the wall. If the light passes through two holes placed side by side, the reflected pattern is not two spots of light but one of alternating stripes of light and shadow. This is thought to be caused by the photons interfering with each other after they pass through the twin holes. So far, this is nothing new. Those of you who took physics in high school probably saw this experiment performed in class.

The newly reported experiment demonstrates that, if the barrier with the two holes is put in place *after the photons have passed by on the way to the wall, they produce stripes of light and shadow just **as if they had** gone through the two holes*. It seems that the photons know in advance what is anticipated of them and form the expected pattern. The significance of the event is clear. Photons in the experiment, being telepathic and precognitive, communicate with the physicist at some level of his being and cooperate with his intent. The physicists contrived a fanciful, complicated explanation of how the striped pattern came about, but I contend that my explanation is the correct one. We are, indeed, part of a living, cooperative Universe.

Intent implies purpose in which an act is initiated for a specific reason. Through their intent, atoms have the ability to make decisions concerning their state of being and, at their level of consciousness, plan for their future. Primarily, intent is directed toward total, joyful cooperation with the Universe and, in specific, with the structure of which it is a part.

Precognition allows an atom to dream, to foresee its future, and make plans accordingly.

Given these essential attributes, it is clear that the Universe is a single, integrated, living entity – that these characteristics are basic qualities of life.

For all these reasons, our perception of mankind must be altered as well. Since we are not standing outside the Universe, watching its goings on as if it were a piece of cosmic machinery running for our amusement and profit, we must admit that we are truly an integral part of the Universe.

Consciousness, awareness, communication, memory, intent, creativity, and precognition are uniformly present throughout the Universe, present at every level of existence from a quantum to a human being. They are what physicists would probably classify as nonlocal connections. Nonlocal connections represent associations between atoms and other bodies that are not ordinarily in some sort of physical relationship or organization with each other. These cosmic connections may act across great distances as we will see. Although these qualities pervade the entire Universe, they usually operate through what might be called "structure units". Starting at the atomic level, let us consider briefly an experiment that was suggested in the early part of the twentieth century.

In the 1930s, Einstein, Podolsky, and Rosen proposed an experiment which would test the characteristics of these nonlocal forces. In discussing nonlocal connections, Niels Bohr thought their actions were instantaneous. Einstein refused to accept the idea that the communication could be instantaneous since he knew that nothing can travel faster than the speed of light. The speed of light as a constant and a maximum was one of the pivotal points upon which his theory of general relativity hinged. If nonlocal connections acted at once, it would violate this principle. Einstein was so adamant in defending his position that he nearly refused to accept the concepts of quantum mechanics – a field of physics that describes the structure of atoms and the motion of subatomic particles. Einstein knew that with modern techniques of measuring minute increments of time, even if the information traveled at the speed of light, it would be possible to measure the time it took for the information to travel from one atom to another. However, when the experiment was proposed, nobody had devised a way to test the theory.

About thirty years later, John S. Bell conducted an experiment proving that Bohr had been correct after all. Nonlocal connections do act instantaneously. Bell's experiment involved communication between two associated atoms and the electrons spinning about them. In paired atoms, electrons spin in opposite directions so that the sum of their spin always totals zero. If one spins clockwise the other always spins counter clockwise. Physicists refer to these directions as being up and down. One can arbitrarily determine the spin of the first atom to be up or down – it doesn't make any difference – and instantly, the electron of the other atom is found spinning in the opposite direction. Knowledge of the direction of spin of the first electron is instantly transferred to the paired atom and its electron. Bell proved that communication between the atoms is immediate even though they might be hundreds or thousands of miles apart or even on opposite sides of the Universe. *There is **no** time lapse.*

Determining the spin of the first electron has no effect on electrons elsewhere – only the one with which it is associated. This paired association constitutes the most simple type of "structure unit".

Today, the velocity of light being the maximum speed that anything can travel is up for question. This was confirmed recently in an experiment by Chiao and others. They demonstrated that under certain conditions photons appear to be going at speeds seventy percent faster than light can travel. So we see that under specific circumstances, it is possible for light to go faster than the supposed maximum of 186,282 miles a second. This concept will be discussed in a later chapter.

As structure units become more complex, the layers of nonlocal connections become equally complex. For example, atoms composing any given molecule only communicate between the atoms in that molecule. Molecules within one cell communicate with each other but not with molecules in other cells. At one level, it can be said that every atom in the Universe is in communication with every other atom, but only indirectly despite it being instantaneous. Therefore, each atom, molecule, cell, and so on, communicates directly within the structure unit to which it belongs.

In the same instantaneous fashion, the other properties, or what might be called the attributes of matter are communicated within the structure units. It is through the properties of awareness and communication that we keep track of our organs, tissues, cells and so on down the structural levels. Atoms, molecules, and cells are aware of their location and purpose. They remember their individual functions by maintaining communication with other elements within the unit. It is loss of communication between cells that causes a cell to attempt to produce a new entity. Through a flawed process, the attempt becomes a malignant growth instead of a clone.[1]

Intent is an attribute of volition and should be considered as totally cooperative in function. Intent is present at every level from a quantum to a Universe. At each level, the purpose of the vaster consciousness supersedes that of the less evolved consciousness. But rather than taking the form of a commanding force, intent coaxes and invites the less evolved consciousness to cooperate for the greater purpose. As a result of this hierarchy of intent, each structure unit is influenced by and cooperates with the purpose of the vaster organization of which it is a part. In this way, during the process of examining subatomic structures such as an electron, the intent of the physicist determines whether the electron will appear as a particle or a wave. The intent of the

---

[1]Confessions of a Healer: MacMurray and Beck 1994

electron is directed toward total cooperation and thereby will not utilize its will for the purpose of defying the wishes of the physicist.

These concepts evolved over time as physicists began to comprehend the behavior of subatomic particles. In the early 1920s, Niels Bohr introduced the concept of complimentarity by stating that the idea of an electron being a particle or a wave were descriptions of the same reality. He also stated, "Isolated material particles are abstractions, their properties being definable and observable only through their interaction with other systems." Later on, Henry Stapp, of the University of California, stated, "An elementary (atomic) particle is not an independently existing, analyzable entity. It is, in essence, a set of relationships that reach outward to other things." It is clear that continued search for the basic building block of matter is an exercise in futility. Subatomic particles are not objects or things but aggregates of intelligent consciousness, interacting with other systems of consciousness that are interacting with other systems. Geoffery Chew came up with the right idea in the mid 1960s when he presented his S-matrix theory of the Universe, commonly known as the "bootstrap" theory. Chew describes the Universe as a web of intertwined psychological events. He denies that any basic particles such as electrons or atoms exist and promotes the idea of a thought construct in which matter and the Universe are based entirely upon the beliefs and the intent of the observer. He also added another dimension which he termed "order" as an aspect or property of subatomic particles. David Bohm speaks much the same way with the concept of an "unbroken wholeness" to describe the Universe. Under the circumstances, I believe we are obligated to accept the truth that the Universe is an integrated, living entity – that awareness, consciousness, communication, memory, precognition, intent, and creativity are basic properties of every quantum, atom, and molecule.

I suspect the problem Einstein had that made it difficult for him to accept the fact that non-local connections were instantaneous was that despite a lifetime of work, developing the theory of general relativity and struggling with the concepts of quantum mechanics, he could not quite break away from the idea that matter and mind were separate as Rene Descartes had proclaimed back in the seventeenth century. I believe he was trapped by his search for some "material" messenger and a mathematical equation to express it. In addition, Einstein could not quite bring himself to say that matter and energy were actually alive – in communication with and responsive to the intent of the observer as well as the entirety of the Universe. I cannot help thinking that, during his final years when he struggled to develop his unified theory, he suspected what the answer was. He almost had to. For some reason, I believe he was unwilling to go out on a limb and state what he surmised to be true. He was not ready to abandon a scientific, mathematical explanation for a philosophical one.

As incarnate entities we identify so completely with our bodies that we tend to relate to only those things that can be perceived through our physical senses. In the biologic state, the mind is fused with the brain and nervous system and total orientation within the body is almost inescapable. Limited as we are in our perceptions, we are not locked away from perceiving other dimensions if we try. Unfortunately, for most of us, if we cannot verify something with our physical senses, we tend to doubt its existence. But, with only the knowledge obtained through our senses, we barely scratch the surface of reality. Scientific instrumentation only enhances what we can see and hear with our eyes and ears and fails to offer any broader view. CT scans, electron microscopes, nuclear magnetic resonance imagery, and radio telescopes for example, are only other ways of seeing.

We have developed instruments for seeing what we believe to be the full range of radiant energy. The extent of our awareness extends from cosmic rays at one end to radio waves at the other end of the spectrum. The divisions we call visible light, radar, infra-red, X-ray and so on are based upon wave length and frequency and are arbitrary separations of a continuum of energy. However, our present concept of radiant energy is almost as limited as it was when we only were aware of visible light and had just our eyes with which to view it. Our knowledge of radiant energy is limited by our concepts and by the limitations of the instruments themselves. Instruments can observe only what they are designed to observe, and their design is limited by the imagination and knowledge of the persons who develop them. I am most certain there are extensions of radiant energy stretching to infinity in both directions beyond cosmic and radio rays. No doubt, there are dimensions extending in other directions. They may be based upon such qualities as thickness, harmonics, breadth of the wave, and speed. This in turn opens the possibility of what have popularly been called alternate Universes structured upon these other dimensions.

Greg tells me that while throwing pots on his wheel he hears music internalized within himself. He transforms the tones into shapes on his potter's wheel. Over forty years ago, I was lying on a sofa in my living room, listening to Beethoven's dramatic Fifth Symphony. I was half asleep when I realized I was "seeing" the music as a three dimensional, abstract form bathed in brilliant colors. The vision lasted perhaps a minute or two and then I lost it. Years later, as I recalled the life of the Chinese seer, I again perceived sound as color. At the same moment I saw the flowers and the earth singing, I was aware that the tones and harmonics were colorful and almost palpable as well as visible. The songs resembled golden columns of honey, having texture, thickness, and substance. One early morning, only a few months ago, I was half awake, dreaming, and I became aware that I was seeing the first movement of Beethoven's Fifth, again. It was so beautiful that it shocked me out of my stupor, and I immediately awoke. The vision burst like a soap bubble with its perfusion of colors. The music of the spheres does exist! Since matter and energy exhibit qualities of consciousness, awareness, communication, memory, intent, creativity, and precognition, the question arises how can an atom of carbon, sodium, or any other element possess these traits? To understand this we have to discuss another aspect of the Universe.

Everything is consciousness – intelligent consciousness. This consciousness is composed of infinitely powerful bits that others have called consciousness-units. Powerful as they are, they have no mass and command no space. They are like points in geometry. Countless numbers are present in each quantum, electron, and so on. It is the consciousness-units that possess these qualities, making matter truly alive. Furthermore, they have the ability to create fields of energy that are electromagnetic in nature. These electromagnetic fields then form other energy fields about them that ultimately become what we refer to as solid matter. What enables the Universe to be a sentient, integrated whole is that it is made of consciousness. Consciousness-units are the basic substance, the true "building blocks", of the Universe.

Consciousness is not some abstract function of the mind or a byproduct of chemical or electrical activity of the brain. It *is* the mind. Furthermore, consciousness (or mind if you prefer that term) is present in everything from interstellar space, stars, rocks, quanta, electrons, plants, animals, and humankind.

Since the Universe is an integrated entity, there are examples of this cooperative integration all about us to be witnessed, even at mundane levels, if we are attentive. Let us consider a couple of examples.

I always marveled at the ability of my attache case to learn how to behave in my car. A new attache case did not know what was expected of it. I would place it on the front seat beside me and it would skid about and fall on the floor at the slightest turn or change of speed. I would replace it in the same spot and position that I had originally put it along with a silent and sometimes angry command to stay put. The sliding about and falling would continue for several weeks. Then, the attache case suddenly seemed to understand. Rarely did it slide about even when I made sharp turns. It never fell off on the floor unless I made a really sudden stop, and then it often managed to hang onto the front edge of the seat and not actually fall. Examination of the attache case revealed no change in the slickness of its surface. It was still as smooth as the day I got it. The car seat was unchanged as well. The attache case had learned its location in space, remembered where it was to stay, and what was expected of it, following the intent of its owner.

Ask any cowboy about the rope he uses to lasso cattle. It takes some time, he'll tell you, before the rope learns how to behave. True, there are changes in flexibility as the rope is used, but when he uses a rope belonging to someone else, it does not behave as well as his own wise one. It is as if the rope is uncertain what the stranger wishes. It requires a lot of learning before the rope knows what to do and how to act. Mankind has so much to learn before it begins to reach its potential. It would be a miracle if we could learn as fast as my attache case or a length of rope. It is man's ego that gets in the way.

For a scientist to look through a telescope, a microscope, or any other instrument in an effort to learn about the Universe and believe he is observing anything other than a very superficial, unbelievably narrow view is foolish indeed. What he learns is not invalid, it is just terribly incomplete. It is not unlike looking at the painted surface of a house and believing you can discern its internal structure and its contents. It does not matter how minutely the paint is examined. It can be analyzed for its various components, its color, surface qualities, durability, and anything else you choose. The fact is that it is merely the paint on the surface, and you are no more aware or knowledgeable of the internal contents or structure of the house than you were at the beginning.

When physicists began their quest for the basic building blocks of matter, they first thought them to be molecules. Then molecules were found to be composed of smaller things called atoms. Finally atoms were "split" resulting in particles with positive and negative electrical charges plus others that had no charge. These particles were called protons, electrons, and neutrons. A whole new field of physics emerged, the study of subatomic particles.

Upon beginning this investigation, a difficulty surfaced. The particles wouldn't behave. They were not found where they were thought to be. Electrons were not spinning around in neat little orbits like planets about the sun as Newtonian principles said they should be. They were flying around the nucleus of the atom, not in flat orbits, but circling about in all directions to produce hollow spheres or shells of energy. Their speed approached that of light. Considering the extremely small diameter of the electron's orbit, coupled with near light speeds, in a sense an electron was everywhere at once. It became evident that to locate an electron one had to calculate the probability of its being at any one place at any one time. This introduced an element of uncertainty into the hard science of physics and mathematics. Certain sciences were designated as "hard" for it was thought that they were based upon hard, irrefutable, unchanging mathematical principles. The "soft" sciences were based upon reason and philosophy. Suddenly, the concept of anything being unchanging or absolute was severely challenged. Accepting the premise that nothing is totally predictable or absolute became a stumbling block for many who were struggling to make sense from a seemingly chaotic situation. It became very like the Eastern concept of how the Universe works. Eastern philosophy, as you recall, embraced the concept of the Universe as a mutable, dynamic balance rather than one of rigid, unchanging laws. Science and philosophy were coming closer and closer together the more the subatomic physicists discovered.

Then the particles themselves turned out to be a paradox. Electrons were both particles and energy waves at the same time. If a scientist set up an experiment to observe an electron as a particle of matter, that is the way the electron appeared. At the same time a scientist might construct another experiment to observe the electron as a wave of energy and it would appear as a wave. The form of the subatomic particle was created by the intent of the physicist. Incidentally, these particles are now thought to be composed of an interplay of minute packets of energy we call quanta – and even quanta have been artificially subdivided into other minute fields of energy known by various names. In recent years, a theory called the "superstring theory" suggests that everything is composed of unbelievably small loops of energy and may account for the various forces in nature.

From the outset, scientific method relied upon the integrity of the unbiased, independent observer. Indeed, the principle of the unbiased observer is considered in the design of every experiment. Now it seemed that the experimenter was an integral part of the experiment and could not be separated from it nor from the end result. Whether he wished it or not, the scientist was in many ways responsible for the outcome of the experiment before it was even conducted. This one thing alone placed mankind and his mind, his desires, and his intent, right back into the thick of the Universe no matter how badly he wished to think of himself as separate from it. ***Descartes failed after all!*** *After "forever" separating mind and matter, they had come full circle and become inseparably enmeshed.* Through his intent, man could make an atomic particle appear as energy or as a form of matter. Man appeared to be, in every sense, a co-creator of the Universe.

Another enigma that distressed the scientists was the concept of time. Time in the Universe is not linear. This means that one event does not necessarily follow the preceding one in an orderly sequence. In the Universe, time is considered "relative" and can be thought of as an enduring present in which all things exist at once in a vast field of probabilities. Even the precepts of Einstein's theory of general relativity state that concepts of "preceding" or "past" depend upon the position of the observer, whether he is moving one direction, or another, or standing still in relation to the event being observed.

Everything is in motion. Even though you may be lying quietly in bed as you read this book, you are in motion. You spin with the Earth on its axis at a speed a bit over 1000 miles an hour at the equator. As it spins, the Earth orbits about the sun while the sun is in constant motion orbiting around the galaxy. Beyond that, the galaxy is in motion within the Universe. For this reason, the measurement of space depends upon where one starts and at what speed and direction you are traveling. Even on Earth, living in linear time, if you and a companion are measuring off four feet on a twelve foot board with the intention of cutting off four feet and ending up with two boards, one eight feet and one four feet, you both need to start measuring at the same end to make your cut.

Speed and position in the cosmos interfere with one another when it comes to measuring them. If you attempt to accurately determine the position of a body in space, the speed at which it is traveling can only be approximated. Conversely, if you calculate the speed precisely, the location can only be estimated. As these concepts were recognized by Einstein, they became part of the theory of general relativity and made time and space dimensions of each other. This dimension came to be called "spacetime".

Time in the Universe can literally go backward as well as forward, or stop. But these ideas still depend upon our notions of space and time which are physical dimensions – dimensions with which we work as incarnate beings. However, from the viewpoint of the Universe, time is "all at once" and not the same as it is for us as biologic, living beings. In a real sense, time in the vastness of the Universe is "timeless".

I was struggling to understand how this "time thing" might work in relationship to incarnations and talked at some length with both Ralph Warner and Greg Satre concerning my dilemma. They both understood the time paradox, but I was having one of my mentally stupid phases and could not grasp fully the meaning of their explanations. One afternoon Greg phoned, saying he had been having a series of visions. The visions were all identical, but he failed to understand their meaning until just then. The vision was that of a tiny speck suddenly enlarged to the size of a huge asteroid where one could walk around and examine every crack, bump, and irregularity on its surface. It was as if someone had suddenly placed the speck under a powerful magnifying glass so that physical irregularities of the surface could be experienced. Suddenly, it came to him that the magnifying glass represented the artifice of linear time. He explained that a lifetime, an incarnational cycle, was like a speck in the Universe or more precisely like a point in geometry. For those of you who do not remember your high school geometry, a point is a place of reference and has no dimension. It has no width, height, or depth. It just is. Linear time acts like a magnifying glass giving the point dimensions that it does not truly possess. It enlarges the speck in relative time to something gigantic so that it can be lived in and examined from all angles.

Viewed from the reality of the Universe, the point has no such features, but through the artificial magnification of linear time, individual incarnations appear to be experienced one after the other. We see them as progressive: cave man, Atlantean, ancient Egyptian, Greek, Celt, Middle European, Puritan, Indian, cowboy, teacher, housewife, and so on. Nonetheless, from the perspective of the Universe, they all occur at once in the enduring present of relative time. This is extremely hard to grasp when viewed from our finite, biological existence, yet on every planet where biologic life forms are evolving, a linear time construction exists. One way to think of this is that throughout the Universe, millions of little "bio-spheres" of linear time are created for the benefit and the development of biologic creatures. Actually, it is through the cooperation of all biologic life-forms that linear time evolved. This is true despite the fact that animals and plants tend to live timeless existences, involved more with the intensity of an event than with the duration over which the event takes place. Linear time is, therefore, a creation of those who experience it.

Einstein and others said it. Matter and energy are actually the same, merely different sides of the same coin. I doubt there is a single knowledgeable person who would debate the truth of this statement: Energy equals Mass times the Speed of light squared. But the equation leads to a paradox. Is something composed of matter or energy? Therefore, it is not appropriate or accurate to speak of matter and energy as separate, since they are one. For this reason, I propose a new term to encompass the dual nature of the matter-energy ambiguity. I will call it "mattergy" and will use the term throughout this book.

Physics and other fields of science are based upon the concept of a singularity – that the Universe is all inclusive. But just because we use that term does not make it a fact. Furthermore, within a singularity, there may be many formats each appearing as a singularity. Over time, we assumed without question the limiting concept of one Universe. For years, I reasoned there had to be more than one. I often speculated about what they might discuss on Saturday night when they got together for a cosmic beer and pizza. While visiting with Ralph Warner about this subject, he informed me that his view of the Universe was quite different from the commonly accepted one. According to his insight, our Universe is limited to what we refer to as the Milky Way Galaxy. Other galaxies are other Universes and distinct from ours.

Greg has a slightly different view. To draw an analogy, when a human entity elects to incarnate, all of the incarnations occur at the same time when viewed from the perspective of relative time. Extensions of each greater human consciousness (oversoul) enter into and fuse with various physical bodies and experience their diverse lives and activities. Greg believes that the same incarnational process occurs at the level of the Universe – that Universes undergo multiple incarnations, as well. The "Supreme Consciousness" of the Universe is analogous with each person's oversoul. For much the same purpose that we enter into multiple incarnations, the Supreme Consciousness participates in billions of incarnational existences. We call these incarnational selves "galaxies". The Milky Way Galaxy is one of those selves. The edge or limit of our Universe is not visible or discernible to us in any way with the knowledge and instruments available to us at this time.

Through meditation, Pan informs me that in addition to our Universe with its billions of incarnational selves there are six other Universes each with billions of incarnational selves. We maintain that all the Universes are contained, or float, within an infinitely vast field of passively alert, undifferentiated consciousness. This field of undifferentiated consciousness along with the Universes may be what Seth referred to as All That Is. As we look outward, we see no boundaries and assume we are looking at untold billions of galaxies within one Universe rather than a number of Universes each with billions of incarnational selves. For those of you who are unfamiliar with Seth, he is the entity channeled by Jane Roberts and who dictated a number of books that were published originally in the 1970s.

Truth, to some degree, always depends upon the position of the observer. In the book *The Caine Mutiny*, the ship's officers were discussing Captain Queeg. One of them remarked that he was an asshole. I recall it was the doctor who said that all ships' captains and others in positions of high authority appeared to be assholes. He reasoned it was the angle from which they were viewed. Like the officers of the Caine we observe things from specific angles and with preconceived notions of what we will see before we look. Most people become rigidly locked into these patterns of thinking and perception. This is particularly apt to occur if they have an interest in achieving a particular outcome for whatever reason.

The fear of reporting the unusual or attempting to step outside conventional thinking has the effect of coercing many scientists into tailoring their investigations and the results to please the individuals handing out grant money and those in control of advancement within the academic field.

A good example of this occurred late in my father's career. He applied for a government grant to fund an original research project that he had in mind. The agency spokesman requested that he submit a letter, stating what the research would reveal. My father replied that he had no idea what this would be since the research had not been done. Indeed, he explained, finding the answer was the purpose of doing the study in the first place. The government spokesman replied that they could not fund a project unless they could be assured of the outcome in advance. In disgust, my father abandoned his effort to obtain the grant.

Many a scientist has been literally "frozen out" of his profession because he dared to investigate or report findings in opposition to accepted beliefs. Rarely does one find an individual who is totally insensitive to these pressures. It is hard to be a purist when the mortgage payment is due, the kids need braces for their teeth, and thousands of dollars of grant money are there for the taking.

It is known that the "form" of subatomic particles is to some degree dependent upon the intent of the observer. Since this is true at the subatomic level, there is no reason why the same principle should not apply elsewhere, indeed, within every field of inquiry. For example, it should affect the observations of astronomers. Every one of their observations is in part created by the intent of the astronomers. By the very act of looking, they create that which they seek. I suspect that at one time or another every astronomer looks through a telescope searching for the outer limits – the edge of the Universe – never considering he may have looked past his own and across neighboring Universes. Perhaps we have searched far enough. Now we need to look in depth or look for other dimensions of reality.

Through his intent, and with the cooperation of the Primary Spiritual Being, man helps create this physical Universe. The specific material appearance or representation of our Universe is created on the basis of mattergy. Elsewhere, other beings might have used sound, color, or dimensions of energy unknown and unperceived by us. As a function and limitation of our biologic form, we are blind to everything that lies beyond our specific construct. Parallel and alternate realities exist side by side, overlapping, or superimposed one upon another, and we are totally oblivious to their presence.

From time to time windows appear which allow us to peek into the other dimensions. An occasional brief sojourn can be made by gifted individuals who have the ability to shift into another dimension. The author, Carlos Castaneda, explains the process being accomplished through the ability to "shift one's assemblage point of perception". One aspect of his training was to learn to change his perception and align himself with alternate realities, or worlds as he referred to them. In this manner, he and others who learned to accomplish this feat could literally step into an alternate reality, vanishing from this one. It is reported that among the Australian aborigines, certain psychically advanced individuals referred to as "time-walkers" can simply vanish "into thin air" and reappear whenever and wherever they please, even hundreds of miles from where they were.

It seems as if these windows between realities can be almost anywhere. I know of one couple living on a farm in Oklahoma who returned home one afternoon only to find their house gone. The out buildings were there, but there was no house, no foundation, nothing. The ground was undisturbed as if no building had ever been there. Understandably, they were terribly upset and drove back to town. When they told their story, they were met by laughter and jeers of disbelief. Realizing they were not going to receive support or understanding by telling their friends about the unnerving experience, they drove back to their farm and found their house where it was supposed to be. Obviously, it had slipped into another dimension for a short while.

Greg Satre relates an event that he experienced as he was driving home to Canon City, Colorado from Albuquerque one star filled night. New Mexico night skies are breathtaking. It was

24

about two in the morning. He had been meditating on the existence of alternate realities when suddenly he became aware that he was no longer on the interstate highway. Everything was absolutely silent. There was no engine noise, no noise of the tires on the road. The headlights were no longer reflecting off the roadside or pavement. He was completely surrounded by stars! There were stars in front, on both sides, below, and in back of him. It was as if he were in deep space. He had driven through a window into an alternate reality, beautiful and awesome. After a span of several minutes he was again on I-25, in the proper lane, heading for home, and everything was back to normal.

I know of a magician who can create windows between alternate realities at will. He uses this ability in his act to make huge objects disappear. He presents the feat as an illusion of magic and, indeed, it is magic, but it is not an illusion. One definition of magic is an extraordinary power or influence, seemingly from a supernatural force. He also has the ability to manipulate energy fields allowing himself to fly, to soar about the auditorium. There is nothing unnatural about what he does. He has simply learned to step beyond the boundaries of the belief system to which we have been conditioned. This allows him to utilize the presence of other dimensions and energies of which most of us know nothing. The primary reason we cannot all do these things is that we do not believe we can. Remember in the Star Wars movie when Luke Skywalker was attempting to levitate his ship from the swamp? He struggled without success and said to Yoda, "I'm trying." To this Yoda responded that was precisely his problem. His command was, "Try not. Do, or do not. There is no try!" It is hard to break the mold of preconceived commitments to reality, perception, and belief.

Occasionally, entities from other dimensions become visible to us. Leprechauns, gnomes, fairies and elves do exist in other realities or worlds. Other so called mythical creatures such as unicorns, mermaids, and centaurs do so as well. Their absence in this dimension is the result of their choosing to enter an alternate dimension for reasons of their own. Folk stories continue to give testimony of their past existence in this world.

One of my American Indian friends told of an event that occurred during a Sun Dance a few years ago. For those who are unfamiliar with Indian ceremonies, the Sun Dance is the most holy, spiritual ceremony practiced by the plains Indians. In recent years, the Sun Dance religion has been adopted by many tribes. I had the good fortune to attend one several years ago, and I can testify it was the most impressive religious ceremony I ever witnessed. I participated in the form of a helper and could not keep tears from flowing down my cheeks as the dance proceeded. It was truly awesome.

My friend told me that on the last day of the dance the "little people" appeared in the Sun Dance pole. There were perhaps a dozen or more about eighteen inches high, running around on the branches and up and down the pole. They ran about on the ground among the dancers. The event lasted several minutes, and just as suddenly as they appeared, they ran up into the pole and vanished. The most interesting aspect of the event was that they were visible to nearly all the people present at the dance including the white people who were spectators. It was not a hallucination of a few, but an event witnessed by many.

The Universe is truly a multidimensional sentient Being of which human development is an integral part. The Universe's multi-dimensionality includes dimensions of alternate and parallel realities as wonderful and awesome as the one with which we are familiar. As with human consciousness, the Universe has chosen to incarnate as myriads of experimental beings and exist in many other forms.

Since "God" and "Universe" are synonyms, when speaking of a multidimensional Universe, we are speaking of a multidimensional God. I have some problems with the term "God" and hesitate to continue using it without some further discussion because it often means something other than what I view as the Primary Spiritual Being. Eons ago, as mankind lost sight of his multidimensional self and cut off communication with the spiritual aspect of the Universe, he could not deny that there was something beyond his person, something vaster than himself. He called this something "God". Over time, he began to ascribe human qualities to this "something". Thus, in a very real sense, a personified concept of God is an idea.

Paul Tillich called God "The Ground of Being", or "Ultimate Concern". He made a distinction between the two by using Ultimate Concern to denote the thing worshiped by a particular person. If the thing of greatest concern to an individual is money or the scientific method, then money or science becomes his personal god. Tillich's term, The Ground of Being, has a deeper, all encompassing meaning. However, his Ground of Being seems to refer only to the spiritual or psychical aspect of God. I doubt Tillich ever conceived of the Universe in its totality being synonymous with his Ground of Being. If he had, I am quite certain he would have spoken of it.

Seth, according to Jane Roberts, uses the phrase "All That Is" to represent God. I am particularly fond of that expression. From our viewpoint, All That Is represents the passively alert field of undifferentiated consciousness and the Universes contained therein. In the purest sense, that is the correct meaning of the term. One way of perceiving our Universe is to think only of the Milky Way Galaxy and its billions of incarnations – and not include the other Universes and their incarnations. To avoid confusion, such terms as Universe, God, All That Is, or Primary Spiritual Being are interchangeable.

CHAPTER 2

The Universe - A Spiritual Being

In an attempt to define spirit, various terms come to mind, all of which mean the same thing. Not surprising, for when we try to describe an experience or an insight of a nonphysical nature, words are often inadequate. In an effort to be accurate, we use words and phrases that have particular nuances of meaning for us. Since each individual relates to a given concept in light of his own unique background of reference, the terms vary. Little wonder, when trying to describe the essence of our being, we use terms like soul, life force, living energy, psyche, entity, and others.

Spirit is intelligent consciousness – a collection of millions of consciousness-units. A spirit does not depend upon a physical body for its existence. It exists with or without physical representation. Unlike the matter/energy paradox in which one is simply an alternate form of the other, *spirit does not evolve as an alternate quality of a physical being.* **Indeed, spirit creates the physical.** A human spirit has dimensions that expand its scope of interaction to degrees that are potentially limitless. Spirit can express and feel love, hate, joy, sadness, remorse, and all the endless nuances of emotion one can conceive. Other living creatures are spirits fused for their sojourn of biologic incarnation as physical forms. Only during an incarnation does any spirit have a physical presence. Contrary to the way we have been led to believe, biological creatures do not have spirits – they are spirits. You do not have a soul. You are a soul. What is more, you cannot lose your soul. To express the concept as an analogy, compare spirit with rain. Rain is composed of innumerable droplets of water, while spirit is composed of untold numbers of consciousness-units. You would not say that rain has water. It would be foolish to think that rain could lose its water. Water is what rain is. It is just as inaccurate and illogical to speak of a person in danger of losing his soul as rain losing its water. A soul could very well lose its body, and does, through the process of dying from disease or injury, but a soul cannot lose itself or become lost. Because we usually are unaware of our other incarnations, we cling to the idea that our body is of primary importance. Therefore, over time, our thinking evolved to the false concept that a human has a soul rather than being one.

The Primary Spiritual Being has a body, too. It is nothing like the bearded, old man painted so beautifully by the master Michelangelo on the ceiling of the Sistine Chapel. Still, we can all admire and honor his painting as a superb and glorious visual metaphor. God is not a discrete, spiritual being located somewhere outside the Universe, responsible for its creation and all it contains. God is in no way separate from His creation. He is the creation.

Metaphorically, we can think of the Universe with its infinite dimensions as the body of God. Keep in mind that the Universe is far more than what we see, looking through our telescopes or gazing at the Milky Way on a clear night. The Universe is composed of all the mattergy, spirit, alternate and parallel realities, and other forms of energy and consciousness that we can only speculate about since we have no way to perceive it.

Mankind, because of the constraints placed upon him by his biologic nature, is more ignorant of the Universe than your pet is of you. Your pet can perceive you and interact with you, but it has no way of comprehending your relationship to the world or the society in which you live. When you read a book or leave the house to go to work, your pet does not have a clue – not even a glimmer of what you are about. Yet, for all we know about the Universe, we are more ignorant of it than your pet is of you.

As ordinarily envisioned, God is an idea. Truth is that God is intelligent consciousness and All There Is. Humankind, as part of the Universe, is therefore part of God. Remember in her movie, *Out On A Limb*, Shirley MacLaine standing in the ocean surf shouting, "I am God!" She was right. You are part of God, as well. You are no more separate from God than a cell deep within your body is separate from you. All consciousness, nonaligned or individuated, is part of God.

God is every star, planet, speck of cosmic dust, and the space between. God is every rock, lake, mountain, river, fungus, amoeba, bacterium, plant, flower, weed, tree, mosquito, flea, dog, louse, fish, wolf, rat, bird, porpoise, elephant, ape, and human being. God is the mold and the cheese that it flavors, the wind of the hurricane, the heat that cooks your food, the virus that causes AIDS, the clouds, the sky in which they float, your most secret thoughts, your fantasies, your dreams, and your fears. God is every race. God is the priest and the prostitute, the seer and the liar, the homosexual and the gay-basher, the saint and the sinner. God is Muslim, Hindu, atheist, Christian, Taoist, Jew, Buddhist, and all others. God is the totality of the Universe down to the last quantum and bit of consciousness – and all that lies between.

The fly you swat is just as much a part of God as you are. The tree you chop down, the weeds you poison in your lawn are the spirit of God incarnate in those particular forms of life. One could just as easily say that a fly or a dandelion is created in the image of God as to say that man is created in His image.

Intellectually, most people would probably come to this conclusion if they could only disentangle themselves from stereotyped thinking and allow themselves to ponder the subject uninhibited by conventional thought. Statements such as a fly being created in the image of God are usually considered to be sacrilegious. Most people would say that you shouldn't even

31

think things like that much less say them. The majority of individuals prefer to believe that only humans have souls and other creatures have something that makes them alive, but that something is not, could not be, a soul. I assure you, it is all made of the same basic stuff whether it is human spirit, mosquito spirit, dandelion spirit, or rock spirit. Certainly, they are different, but the main difference lies in the degree of their interactive potentials and in the vastness of their spiritual relationships.

Nonhuman spirit of minerals, plants, and animals varies widely in its level of involvement in the Universe. But regardless of its apparent plane of interaction, it can be thought of only as unidimensional. As we have been taught to think, a gorilla has a greater capacity for visible emotion and intelligence than does a tree or an earthworm, but a gorilla is still singular in his dimensionality. Each living entity, however, has the potential for a full range of emotion albeit extremely rudimentary in the less evolved forms.

Human spirit is more highly evolved than that of rocks, animals, and plants. One can think of it as being constructed in a different fashion. Therefore, it is not man's ability to reason that sets him apart from animals, for animals have the faculty of reason as well. It is not the development of an upright stance, an opposing thumb, the shape of the molars, the size of the frontal lobes, a hyoid bone, the development of vocal speech, or any other physical trait that makes mankind unique from other biologic forms of life thus rendering it human. When anthropologists cite the various anatomical and functional differences between prehistoric creatures, apes, and men, they delude themselves. They assume that physical structure and function are what determine whether a creature is human or not. One anthropologist stated that since men and chimpanzees were so closely related genetically, and considering all the time that has elapsed, he did not understand why chimpanzees had not evolved into men. This scientist was obviously missing the entire point. It is man's multidimensional spirit giving him the capacity to be involved in other dimensions of the Universe at a multitude of different levels of interaction that separates mankind from animals, plants, and minerals. Physiologically and anatomically the human body sprang from the same biologic line as apes, but man's spirit did not. Human consciousness is a totally unique form of spiritual energy.

The sum total of all spirit forms of plants, animals, and humans on this and all the other planets, and parallel and alternate realities contribute to and are part of the spirit of God. To this we must add the spirit that constitutes all the so-called nonliving parts of the Universe: water, rocks, minerals, air, cosmic dust, stars, and so on. Do this, and we have some idea of the vastness of the Primary Spiritual Being. The enormous empty expanses between stars and galaxies are not actually empty. This space is filled with intelligent consciousness. It is quite apparent that the Universe is more complex than we think and more vast than we can conceive. All these things and beings are but extensions of energy included within the spirit of the Universe. If we think of human spirit as multidimensional then the spirit of the Universe is infinitely dimensional.

The Primary Spiritual Being is perpetually evolving, learning, and incarnating. On the large scale, new galaxies are constantly being formed in which the Universe experiments with other lines of probable reality. Within the center of each galaxy, and elsewhere, are black holes where mattergy is absorbed and realigned. At the same time, new stars and planets are created as mattergy spews out of the other side which can be called "white holes". Lately, astronomers have come up with a theory that quasars are the white-hot ends of cosmic tubes the other ends of which are black holes. Each black/white hole actually functions as a torus in which mattergy is taken in one side and poured out the other in a constant, cosmic, reincarnation of consciousness. By definition, a torus is a doughnut shaped geometric form that is generated by a circle and rotates about an axis that is perpendicular to the plane of the circle. The Universe was not created through some sort of "Big Bang" as it is popularly stated. What we fail to understand is that the Universe is perpetually creating itself at every point of its being on a moment to moment basis.

On the smaller scale and perhaps a bit easier to grasp, when a tree dies its spirit enters a sapling of the same species. Cats and dogs reincarnate as cats and dogs, elephants as elephants, and so on. But, ultimately, even the spirits of animals are not limited in their development for they have the capacity to unite and create new entities. The hyena is a good example.

Since spirit has memory, it carries the accumulated knowledge from generation to generation. This information is also retained in the bio-consciousness and passed on by the consciousness-units in the reproductive cells. Furthermore, every cell in the Universe is in communication with all other cells. Part of this transmitted knowledge is known as instinct. The less evolved spirits found in animals and plants apparently have little trouble recalling knowledge and behaviors learned in previous incarnations. In this way, cats and dogs remember how to be cats and dogs and behave accordingly.

Since humans have few spiritual memories of which we are consciously aware, we generally rely upon our intellect. That alone puts many of us at a great disadvantage. First of all, most of us are not nearly as intelligent as we would like to think. In the second place, we rarely use our intellect to the same relative capacity as do the other forms of life.

All living entities express emotions that are appropriate to their level of development. To the degree with which they are capable, they fear, hate, love, become angry, and so on. All these qualities that we assume to be uniquely human emotions can be found at some degree of development in all biological creatures. While an earthworm does not fall in love, fear, or hate as we do, it is conscious, and aware, and knows all that is required for its existence. It will react to its environment and to other worms with the full power of its capability, limited though it may be.

Incidentally, those gorillas and chimpanzees that have been taught to communicate using sign language have shown conclusively that they are capable of a very high level of reasoning and emotions such as love, compassion, grief, fear, and dread. Many people refuse to accept these things. Their egos will not allow them to consider that other creatures think, have preferences, feelings, and rights. Then, too, most of us would prefer to think of them as dumb animals for it makes it easier to cage them, to perform experiments on them, and to treat them in callous, cruel ways – supposedly for the benefit of man.

Plants have been studied extensively for their response to physical injury and their interaction with humans. No doubt everyone has heard of experiments in which plants grew better when classical music was played to them, while similar plants failed to thrive and even died in an environment of hard-rock music. Other experiments reveal that plants grow better when people speak to them with kindness. These observations are not fantasy but the result of well documented, carefully controlled studies. Often, we scoff at these reports for we prefer not to believe that plants having feelings. We do not like to think of our house plants screaming in agony as they die of thirst when we forget to water them or go on vacation, leaving no one to assume responsibility for their care.

Some of the most exciting experiments performed in the United States concerning the spiritual nature and the knowing awareness of plants were done in the 1960s by Cleve Backster. Backster was an expert in the use of lie detectors.

Out of curiosity, Backster placed electrodes on the leaf of a philodendron sitting on his desk. Philodendrons happen to be highly active plants. He attached the wires from the electrodes to a polygraph, and observed the electrical gradient between the upper and lower surface of the leaf to produce a wave with a consistent pattern and rhythm. This proved interesting, so he set out to see what, if anything, would alter the wave pattern. He cut a leaf with scissors and the plant reacted with a wild fluctuation of energy potential. Using his cigarette lighter, he burned a leaf. The polygraph reacted in the same dramatic fashion as when he cut it. He relit the lighter, and the closer the flame got to the plant the greater the fluctuations became. Then he made a startling discovery, as if the preceding was not astonishing enough. Merely thinking about burning the plant, not even lighting the lighter but just thinking of doing so, produced the same response as if he had actually burned it. It was not quite as dramatic as when he actually burned it, but a response was produced every time.

Backster found when he gave the plant water and fertilizer, the reaction was dramatic, as well, but in a different wave pattern than when it was injured or threatened. He also discovered that the plant reacted differently in the presence of different people. It responded to individuals who liked plants with the same pattern as when it was given water or food. People who did not like plants caused a response more like an injury.

He also observed that the plant responded to the injury of other creatures. To document this, he set up an experiment. He attached a philodendron to a polygraph, and in an adjoining room, a machine was constructed that dropped a few brine shrimp into boiling water at haphazard times. Each time some shrimp were killed, the philodendron responded with a change in its electrical potential. This response occurred regardless of the presence of humans. Backster's experimentation with plants went on for years, and many other scientists throughout the world documented similar results, as well.

A gifted psychic will tell you that plants communicate with each other. It is known that when a potato plant is attacked by potato bugs the plant exudes a chemical that is toxic to the insects. The chemical serves as a defense mechanism to prevent and minimize further damage. Recently, botanists reported that the affected plant communicates with other potato plants that have yet to be attacked, and those plants start producing the same chemical thus helping to ward off the bugs in advance.

The clear cutting of forests during logging operations is an obscenity in itself, but one of the worst effects occurs when the ancient trees are removed. As young trees sprout, or are planted, in the denuded area, there is much anxiety among them because there are no old trees around. Due to their high level of intelligence and the many years required to reach maturity, saplings require nurture and guidance as they grow and develop. Under ordinary circumstances they receive this guidance from older trees. The young ones, for example, are warned of impending dry seasons and instructed to send their tap roots deeper. Advice is given concerning how much to close the stomata of their leaves to conserve moisture. When rains come, the young trees are cautioned not to take up too much water. Overloading with water makes their limbs heavy and more easily broken by the wind. Many adjustments that trees make to the environment are actually learned behaviors. Like humans, knowledge can be attained more quickly if there are older ones to give instruction. It sounds strange to speak of trees and other plants in this fashion when humans are locked into a belief in which only they emote, have intelligence, communicate, and have memories.

Any credible psychic can tell you the same things that Backster and others documented in various experiments. These spiritual or emotional responses are present in all biological creatures from bacteria to humans. Man is only different – not superior – from other living creatures, but so is every other creature different in its unique way. Difference does not imply superiority. This is important! Difference does not imply either superiority or inferiority. It never does. Mankind has fallen into a trap of the ego's making. We see other creatures or people to be dissimilar and judge them inferior. Unfortunately, many of us do not go about our business of being a human being as well as an earthworm does being a worm. Your pet may be fulfilling its purpose as a dog, or a cat, or a canary far better than you are fulfilling yours as a human being. Even a rock knows how to be a rock and fulfills its purpose and its destiny with magnificence. Such a view is not a very flattering concept for your ego to accept, but it may be alarmingly close to the truth.

One of the reasons animals, plants, and rocks perform their function within the Universe so well is that they understand and accept their position within the system. It seems obvious that beings, other than man, have a clear, inalterable concept of their purpose. An oak tree knows exactly how to behave. It does not, for instance, attempt to act like a pine tree, nor does it stand about wishing it had been a pine and thus live its life in a continual state of discontent. An oak is delighted to fulfill its destiny by just being itself. Certainly, there are fewer degrees of freedom available to trees, flowers, flies, and dogs. Obviously their thought processes are far simpler and quite different than are the thought processes of man. Nonetheless, to the degree of which they are capable, all life forms do think, plan, anticipate, dream, and have reasoning capabilities appropriate to their need. This is true of all matter, right down to the last electron in a grain of sand.

A leopard, when presented with the problem of how best to catch an antelope, has the ability to discern the approaches available to her and, by reason, choose the one that offers the greatest opportunity for success. Once the problem is solved and the decision made, she ceases to think about the other approaches and goes about the business of stalking her prey. She does not worry about what might happen nor does she second guess herself.

Through the properties of consciousness, awareness, memory, and communication, all biologic entities maintain contact within their own species and with the Universe. For example, there is a bond of communication existing between all plants. There is another bond between trees, another between grasses, another between flowers, and so forth. At a more specific level, there is communication between all oak trees, a separate one for pine trees, another for maple trees, and so on.

38

Activity within these communication bonds, which are the nonlocal connections previously described, can be documented as waves of electrical potential within the individual plants. Many years ago, Dr. Harold Saxton Burr, in his book *The Fields of Life*, told of an experiment he conducted in which electrodes were inserted in the trunk of a maple tree on the campus of Yale University, and forty miles away in Old Lyme, Connecticut, the same was done with an elm tree. For a number of years, changes in the electrical potential of each tree were recorded along with the changes of electrical potential between the earth and the tree, within the earth itself, and between the earth and the atmosphere. He found varying rhythms of electrical potential present in the trees corresponding with day-night cycles, seasons of the year, lunar cycles, solar flares, and thunder storms. The trees' cycles were always in phase with the changes in the atmosphere, seasons, sun, moon, and earth. There were two wave patterns identified by the computer that he could not correlate with anything they were studying. These were likely due to patterns of changing potential brought about by communication between all plants and the other between trees.

No creature is isolated. Every biologic entity exists within a community of similar entities and they within a greater community of all living things. Within these communities there is support, instruction, guidance, and comfort, all in keeping with the specific level of consciousness present within the species. In addition, biologic creatures can communicate with creatures of different species. This was demonstrated by Backster when the philodendron reacted to the death of the brine shrimp and to his thoughts.

When I practiced medicine, I was constantly reassessing my medical knowledge in relation to the things I was learning about the Universe. The accomplishment of this never ending process required a tremendous amount of attention and time. In addition, the effort of keeping up with my profession, the stresses of practice, and the politics of the medical community gave me some difficulty sleeping from time to time. In my home, I had a huge Boston fern. I acquired it as a tiny plant with just three fronds, and it grew into a mature fern a good six feet in diameter. We were friends. It stood on a fairly tall pedestal in my living room. On many occasions, I would get out of bed and go to the living room and sit beneath my fern. There I would sort through my problems and the concepts I was attempting to integrate into my belief system. Doing so, in the company of my wise friend, always gave me a sense of great peace as the worry and concern seemed to evaporate. The fern, as would any true friend, understood my torment and discontent and absorbed my fatigue, uncertainties, and anguish unto itself.

Mankind has much to learn from other biological entities. At the present time of human development we are beginning to observe and learn, but we have not explored beyond the level of considering what uses the other creatures may offer in supplying material for our needs. Presently, we are disturbed about the destruction of the rain forests especially in terms of drugs or chemicals that may be undiscovered before the forest is destroyed. This is a worthy concern, but perhaps deeper and more profound lessons could be learned about life in general and how diverse biologic entities can live in perfect balance. Questions such as these are not incapable of being studied. We only need to continue the ecological studies already begun and extend them to deeper levels of consciousness. We need be reminded, as well, that the lessons will be learned only from living beings. A dead tree or plant can teach very little.

There is an old Chinese fable about a tree that was good for nothing. It did not bear fruit. Its trunk and branches were crooked and could not be used for lumber. So, the totally useless tree grew beside the path for hundreds of years. Birds built their nests in its branches. Its foliage was beautiful to behold in the fall season, and it gave shade to weary travelers who paused to rest beneath its branches. The tree was of great value, as a tree. It was of no value to those who perceived a tree only as something to be used for purposes other than a tree.

A little wild flower presented a great lesson to me one year. During the time I practiced medicine in Bellaire, Ohio, one of my responsibilities for a period of time was to help staff in one of our branch clinics a few miles down the Ohio river in the town of Powhatan. The only road between the towns ran along the river. Some major rebuilding of an underpass took place that year. There was little space along the river so detours were impossible. Consequently, traffic was required to stop while heavy equipment moved across the roadway and work was being done. Usually there was a delay of five or ten minutes each time traffic was stopped.

Early in the spring, as I was halted by the road block, I noticed a little patch of ground beside the highway that had somehow been left undisturbed by the bulldozers. All about that one small bit of ground that was no more than a foot or so across were slabs of broken concrete, boulders, and masses of upturned soil. In the middle of the tiny patch, amid chaos all about, was a single plant. Its leaves were dusty, but there it was, growing straight and tall, undisturbed by the destruction.

Twice a week on my way to Powhatan I observed the plant. It continued to grow and thrive. August came and beautiful blue flowers burst forth from its buds. Bees collected pollen on their bodies and pollinated the flowers as they walked about seeking nectar. Eventually, the flowers withered, leaving seed pods. By November the little plant had completed its life cycle and died in a severe frost, but the seeds had scattered, insuring its continuation into the next season. The little plant had pulled it off! It won! With its world ripped asunder, it persisted, quietly fulfilling its purpose and its destiny.

In his retirement speech, as he was leaving the University of Illinois, my father confessed that he used to worry about being a success. He said that one very hot day he was resting in the shade of a truck at the university experimental farm, talking with his friend and colleague, Wayne Beaver. They decided they probably

41

would never amount to anything and might as well quit worrying about it and just go about their business, doing their daily job. It was shortly thereafter that my father began the specific line of morphological research that eventually led to his being awarded a Gugenheim Fellowship.

Viktor Frankl was an existential philosopher and a Nazi death-camp survivor. Through his philosophy, he helped a number of prisoners survive the ordeal. After the war's end, he wrote several books, outlining his experiences and beliefs. I once attended one of his lectures. He stated that happiness and success were like doves that land upon your shoulder. The doves will be content to remain as long as you do not attempt to capture and to possess them. Moreover, happiness and success are usually attained by going quietly about the business of doing one's daily job.

Most people, placed in a similar situation as the little plant on Route 7 in Ohio, would have worried themselves sick or launched into a futile attempt to control the chaotic events occurring about. Because of our capacity to wonder and to speculate, we often lose touch with our center and thus lose sight of our true goal – being human and attaining wisdom.

In the delightful book, *The Tao of Pooh*, Pooh is visiting with the author, Benjamin Hoff. They observe Rabbit running about full of self-importance and not paying attention to what they are trying to say to him. Pooh remarks that Rabbit has brain and that he is smart. To this Hoff agrees. Then Pooh observes, "That must be why he never seems to understand anything."

I knew a doctor who graduated two years ahead of me. After doing research for several years, he entered private practice in internal medicine. He was very learned and derived a lot of pleasure demonstrating to others just how much he knew. To prove it, he quoted medical literature at length and there was not a one of us who was unimpressed. Truly, he was very intelligent and a nice guy, but he was a total failure as a physician. In short, when it came to putting his knowledge to use, he wasn't very smart at all, and he understood little if anything about practicing medicine. After a year, he went back to research. Often his problem is our problem, as well. Like Rabbit, we let our brains and our cleverness get in our way of understanding life and accomplishing our primary task.

The term "center" which I have used needs some explanation. It is an Eastern concept and more specifically a Zen Buddhist one. The term concerns the point of balance in which the individual attains a state of reconciliation or harmony with the paradoxical forces of life. Some refer to this state as attaining one's "still point". Eastern philosophy understands that to be rigidly positioned is incompatible with life. As one walks upon a balance beam, there is constant pull of gravity first one way and then the other. To be rigid is to fall. To maintain balance, one must be flexible. The term center has also crept into the English language. We speak of an individual as being self-centered, eccentric, or well-centered. In doing so, we use the term with much the same meaning as do Buddhists. Center refers to the Essence of your Essential Being or, if you prefer, your soul.

When I was practicing medicine, I observed that most of my patients had no true sense of their center. Their egos were caught up with things, activities, and relationships to the point that they identified themselves almost exclusively with those external attachments. When asked to state who they were in two or three sentences, they usually replied with statements indicating that they were a mother, a farmer, a wife, a coal miner, or even the captain of their bowling team. Rarely did anyone reply that they were a human being.

I urged my patients to perform an exercise on a daily basis, taking perhaps ten minutes of their time. I asked them to sit quietly in a chair and imagine they were at the center of a circle. The periphery of the circle, five or six feet away, was composed of everything with which they were involved or identified. Thus, Jane Jones would push out to the periphery: the Mrs. Jones, her husband and children, her parents and in-laws, her job, her home, her possessions, her friends, her religion, her health, her looks, beliefs about herself, others' beliefs about her, and any other attachments Jane had made. Then she was to reflect upon those things and associations out at the periphery until she came to realize that they were not "Jane", only associations or attachments that Jane had made. The more successful Jane was in separating the Essence of Jane from everything she placed out at the edge of the circle, paradoxically the more freedom she possessed to become involved with them. Separated from these external attachments, her ego was no longer on the line. She could fail or succeed in any or all of these involvements without affecting the basic core of her being.

I told my patients that the ultimate goal of the exercise would be attained when someone could come to them and say, "You have been fired from your job. Your spouse and children have all been killed in an auto accident. Your house burned down, destroying everything you owned. Your parents, in-laws, and friends have turned against you. Everything you believed true has been proven false. You have been excommunicated from your church. The bank failed, leaving you penniless. Your bowling league won't let you wear your team shirt. The doctor says you have an incurable illness and only a month to live." To all this, my patient could reply, "So far, nothing has happened to me. The Essence within me, my soul, the real me, is still intact."

Thus, free of her ego's involvement, Jane is able to become even more involved with her activities if she chooses to do so. If her children succeed, her joy is for them and their success and not because their triumph adds to her inflated ego. If they fail, she is there to help rather than respond with, "How could you shame me so?" To outsiders, Jane may appear no different than before. They may notice a lack of frantic, egocentric concern in her life. There may be fewer lines of worry and desperation on her face. To the outsider, Jane will probably appear quite unchanged. But, she will have learned the joy of freedom and the fun in the challenges life offers. She will have become centered.

44

Once man comprehends that he is a spiritual entity living as a body and one with the Primary Spiritual Being, he must come to grips with the fact that all biological creatures are the same. In fact, at another level of existence, even the Earth and the stars are spiritual entities. All mattergy, you will recall, is alive. Acceptance of this fundamental principle demands a change of attitude and behavior. Many so-called primitive people hold beliefs and attitudes far more mature and wise than do educated individuals from highly technical cultures. Technological success and development does not ensure that the society or the individual has evolved spiritually. Indeed, a good argument can be made that technology may render mankind insensitive to its true nature. Nor does education guarantee that an individual is wise or has motives of a higher spiritual nature. On the other hand, the most uneducated, unsophisticated person may possess great wisdom, understanding, and compassion for others. As we pursue the "game" of science and learning, our egos often become so dazzled by the glitter of our scientific accomplishments that we are blinded to philosophical thought and spiritual meaning. In many ways, the more we achieve the greater our loss.

Years ago I visited Italy. One day, while riding on a bus from Florence to Rome, I noticed an old lady carrying water from the village pump to her home. The village was on a steep hillside and the pump was a great many feet below the level of her house. She was laughing and talking with a friend as she climbed the steps carrying two buckets of water. I thought how difficult it must be to have to climb that hill each time she needed water. Certainly, having a pump to bring water directly to her home would save her time, not to mention the hard, steep climb.

Thinking about this started me reflecting about labor saving devices of all kinds. Of course, it would be easier for her to have a pump, but it would cost her a great deal. No longer would she need to make the steep climb, and she would miss the exercise. Her cardiovascular fitness had to be tops. She would miss visiting with her friend and the companionship that was surely

45

present when the women gathered about the pump, waiting their turn to fill their containers. Furthermore, fetching water is a chore with a very clear, direct purpose. Having purpose in one's life is of great importance even if that purpose is only to fetch water. Indeed, having a pump would have been convenient and easier, but it would not have added one iota of meaning to the woman's life.

Traditionally, American Indians were true Taoists in their understanding and approach to life. They saw themselves as part of, not separate from, the Universe. Many Indian tribes, when forced to go onto reservations through starvation and loss of habitat, were repulsed by the thought of farming and refused to do so. They believed the Earth to be a living being and would no more willingly plow up the Earth to plant crops than to rip open their mothers' bodies. They believed the Earth and all living creatures to be partners and brothers in the Universe.

Prayer before the hunt, for example, was a petition for the animals to understand the need of the hunter for food and to gain the animals' cooperation and permission to take their lives. The outcome of the hunt was dependent upon the success of the prayer in gaining the cooperation of the animals. This is far different than simply praying for good luck so one can successfully kill game, regardless of the need.

I do not propose that we cease killing other creatures. All living creatures kill other beings for survival. I do not suggest we quit building roads or farming the land. Nor do I oppose raising animals for their fur as long as they are well treated and humanely killed.[1] I do suggest that we evaluate our need to do what we do and to perform only those acts that are truly required. When we tear into the earth, cut down trees, catch fish, and kill animals for food – all these things – we should do them with restraint and

---

[1] I am opposed to trapping wild animals. Killing a wild, free animal is quite different than killing one that has never known an existence outside a cage and has been raised for a specific purpose.

46

reverence. Like the members of many "primitive" cultures, we should reverently ask the Earth and the creatures for forgiveness, understanding, and cooperation. Imagine how different the world would be if mankind adopted this attitude.

The Universe is a spiritual entity composed of consciousness. From our perspective we are generally aware of three forms of consciousness: human, animal, and plant. Clearly, we must add a fourth, that of so called nonliving things like rocks and minerals. Spirit is not mattergy. Spirit creates mattergy and reality. In the last chapter I spoke of structure units and explained that intent is a factor which operates in sort of a chain of command. In this way, a cell through its intent influences the molecules of which it is composed.

Intent does not impose or force its influence as much as it invites participation through which other consciousnesses can pursue creativity and a potential of being that otherwise would lie beyond their solitary means. Since freewill operates throughout, fundamental formations and alliances of consciousness are voluntary, creative, and cooperative on a mutual basis. Joyful participation toward creative opportunity is the basis of behavior when intent directs the action. This does not imply any coercive influence. There is the strength of wisdom which is freely followed and based upon recognition of a vaster view. This acknowledgement leads and entices the chief purpose toward creative exploration and value-fulfillment at every level.

This is the way spirit creates its physical environment from mattergy. The statement that God created the Universe and man creates his own environment is not new. But it would be more accurate to say the spirit of God and the collective intent of all biologic and non-biologic kinds of existence formed/forms the physical Universe.

Remember, the Universe is intelligent consciousness actualized by intent. I stated that in the first chapter. It was so important that I made an entire paragraph in bold italics out of that one sentence. Do not forget the physics experiment in which the scientist literally creates a particle or a wave of energy by the manner in which he structures the experiment to observe the electron. In a sense, he says, "I want you electrons to be particles." So, by his intent, he designs the experiment to show them as particles. They do not turn up as waves of energy because his intent enticed them to be particles, and through their intent they cooperate.

To state again, the physical Universe as we perceive it was/is created by the collective intent of all biologic and nonbiologic forms of spirit coupled with the cooperative intent of the Primary Spiritual Being. Eons ago they gradually settled upon what form the Universe would take. The combined intent of every quantum and creature from rocks, plants, animals and men literally decided which form and structure was preferred. Since its form is fairly stable, spirits entering the Earth plane now have little choice. If they want to participate on the Earth, or any other structure for that matter, they must agree to the form and the design of that reality. They don't have to participate in any specific structure, but value-fulfillment and creative development are primary goals of consciousness. Therefore, they are willing to follow the rules that make a given reality format possible, creative, and fulfilling.

In a sense, all incarnated beings "buy the package" when they embark on any incarnational venture the same way they accept the artifice of linear time. Individual intent cannot overrule the tremendous mass of psychic energy that holds the creation in a state of relative stability. Therefore, we must pound nails into boards to hold them together. We must open doors to go through them. And little children can play jump-rope secure in the belief that they will not go floating off into space each time they leave the ground.

Now, if enough people got together and collectively altered their intent in another direction, they could change the world. It has happened. This is one explanation for the creation of some alternate realities. There is plenty of material with which to work. Nonaligned consciousness is all about. By our intent it can be structured any way we choose.

Psychics are gifted individuals who have the ability to step beyond the bounds of collective perception and standard accepted belief systems. The gifted ones can tap into what Jung referred to as the collective unconscious and the Hindu call the akashic records and retrieve information ordinarily unavailable to others at conscious levels. Some psychics, like my friends, are true seers, able to alter their perception to view physical objects and people as scintillating fields of energy. They perceive the consciousness of the Universe in wondrous ways. They are not alone when they state that several alternate realities exist, one of which is so "close" to ours that it touches and overlaps ours in places. In a time long past, before the form of this Universe was so solidified, many life forms, acting through their collective intent, simply constructed other realities. They chose to align themselves with a different one and, after death in this dimension, reincarnated in the new one or, at times, stepped out of this one into the other.

CHAPTER 3

The Multidimensional Spirit

Consciousness is the basic substance of everything: a rose, a wolf, a grain of sand, interstellar space, a human being. By discussing consciousness in its various forms, much light will be shed on the subject of multiple incarnations. It will also become evident that constant development and change are essential functions of the Universe in its creative ventures. Creativity in itself implies and demands change.

As previously explained, the entirety of the Universe is made up of a limitless number of infinitely small foci of energy called consciousness-units. These tiny bits are, indeed, conscious and exhibit properties of communication, awareness, memory, intent, creativity, and precognition. There is a tendency for our minds to balk at the idea that something that cannot be seen or measured can be real and possess these qualities. Still, we know that thoughts are real and have the power to influence others and bring about profound changes in our lives and in the environment. We do not demand that some method be devised to quantify them or demonstrate their presence to prove that thoughts actually exist. Perhaps, like Tao, we can only talk about spirit rather than speak of it for it eludes definition, description and, to a large degree, comprehension. Spirit might be compared to water. Water can exist as liquid, ice, vapor in the atmosphere, or bound in many chemical compounds. We can speak with confidence about the various types of vessels in which water can be stored. We can describe the process of pouring it from one container to another. We can even say that it feels wet, or that it is hot or cold. All this can be done without ever knowing the chemical structure of water itself.

Perhaps a good way to understand spirit is to consider how it came to be. Those of you who are familiar with the teachings of Seth as channeled by Jane Roberts will recognize the common basis of some of the information presented. This is not surprising, for the closer any of us come to the Truth, the more our descriptions resemble one another. Admittedly, we are attempting to describe the same multidimensional Truth. The reader should know that the first draft of this book was written before I read Jane Roberts' books. My friend, Ralph Warner, urged me to read them, but for some reason, I never got around to it. Finally, after reading them, I was amazed to discover that I held many of the same beliefs all my life. Numerous insights were given to me during the writing of this manuscript through intuitive flashes and dreams. Many were identical in substance to those given by Seth.

Whether the following discussion is thought of as a metaphor, a myth, or an account of what actually occurred is of no great importance. The important thing is to grasp the underlying concepts. Facts, after all, are myths that have gained universal acceptance.

Insofar as we know, there has never been a time when the consciousness that is the Universe did not exist. The "Big Bang" theory is at best a very superficial concept that only addresses certain physical aspects of the Universe. Moreover, the theory is based upon calculations that now are thought by many to be inaccurate. Neither does it take into account that the Universe exists in relative time rather than sequential time.

The Universe is ever growing and changing, so what might be considered a rather thorough understanding at this moment will be incomplete in the future. The Universe, in every sense of the word, is constantly restructuring and reinventing itself on a moment to moment basis. It exists in a state of constant creation at all points of its being. The Universe is made of intelligent consciousness and cannot be defined in physical terms alone. Nor can consciousness be enclosed in a neat package, wrapped in dogma, and tied with the ribbon conventional thought. In short, we have no way of determining the vastness or the nature of the Universe, and we never will. Indeed, only about six percent of consciousness is present in any physical manifestation. Like the visible portion of an iceberg that protrudes above the ocean's surface, an electron or an atom represents only a tiny portion of the vast field of consciousness that constitutes and supports its existence. Seth stated that if consciousness took up space, then the consciousness making up a single cell would command an expanse as large as the Earth.

If we can grasp the way by which we create our everyday reality, it will help us understand the Universe. Beyond this, understanding the mechanism is critical to comprehending life and its paradoxes. To that end, try this little mental exercise, keeping in mind that thoughts are real things that exist forever as electromagnetic fields.

Imagine that all the people, activities, and material things that surround you are not physically there. Envision, if you will, that they exist simply as desires, plans, ideas, and fantasies – probabilities that reside in your thoughts. Therefore, you are not propped up in bed or sitting in a chair, reading this book. You are imagining that you are reading an imaginary book propped up in an imaginary bed or chair. Once you accomplish this mental flip-flop, accept a new belief that reality exists only as ideas and thoughts in your mind. Further assume that these infinite possibilities – all the things that could be – form a vast psychological network, a syncytium of probabilities, consisting of all past, present, and future actions, constructs, events, concepts, myths, and fantasies. These probabilities form the basic framework of consciousness that is the Universe – the true

Universe. Using the term channeled from Seth, we will call this psychological reality of probabilities Framework II.

Now you are ready to take the next step in the creation of your day to day physical environment of things and events. This transient, everyday existence in which we live and interact is called Framework I. We create it from the available options, existing in Framework II. Keep in mind that consciousness creates reality and form rather than form developing consciousness. Our daily reality consisting of things and activities comes into being through the process of selecting certain probabilities from Framework II and, through the focus of our intent, actualizing them into reality in this dimension, Framework I.

There are several steps to the process. The electromagnetic fields of which thoughts are composed have the ability to organize energy fields about them. These in turn form other energy fields that we perceive as matter. This process is triggered by our intent. We do this so automatically and so easily on a moment to moment basis that we are completely unaware of the process. The statement that all things exist in thought reminds one of the often quoted words of Rene Descartes, "I think therefore I am". In this, at least, Descartes was correct.

To give an example, if you have an idea for a new gadget of some kind, the invention exists first as a concept, a thought-construction in your mind. Once conceived, the thought becomes part of Framework II and will remain there forever whether you decide to produce the first prototype or not. When you manufacture it of metal, plastic, and so on, you make it a reality in Framework I. Doing so, it becomes a Framework I reality for everyone else. In the meantime, any variations of your invention that you or others may have considered exist in Framework II, as well. These changes bide their time, waiting to become manifest in Framework I should someone choose to actualize them.

This process is not limited to physical objects. When you arise in the morning, every probability of action awaits you. You could elect to go back to sleep. You could go to work or drive across the country to visit a friend. You might walk to the post office, step in front of a speeding car, or drive off a bridge. The probability exists for you to read a book, bake cookies, go fishing, mow the lawn, visit with your spouse, or whatever comes to mind. Probabilities are endless. All potentials of action and attitude exist in Framework II, awaiting your selection. Once your decision is made, that probability becomes reality in Framework I through the steps already mentioned. Clearly, every action, thing, or idea exists as a probability in Framework II before it exists in the reality of our physical world.

Beyond Framework II lie other Frameworks of consciousness. Framework III contains the consciousness fields that form and modify the probabilities in Framework II. This includes concepts, associations, and relationships of beliefs and ideas. Entities working in Framework III create and juxtapose various combinations of ideas to be tried out in Framework II. Metaphorically, a Framework III guide may gather up a concept expressed as a tone, a harmonic, or a color and compress it to produce a nidus or an aggregate of ideas, trying it out in combination with other values to create a new concept or a new conceptual experience. This new concept is introduced into Framework II independently, or attached to other probabilities residing there, altering and modifying them. In this way, the new concepts may be shared with Framework II and remain available to be tested in Framework I or in alternate or parallel realities of Framework I.

The symbolism in Framework III is different than that of Framework II and must be translated, as do the others, before it can be understood. In Framework III, information is coded as electromagnetic fields similar to the way information is stored on a magnetic tape or transmitted by fiber-optic cable. These probabilities are fluid and mutable, and when viewed by us appear as colorful clouds, sounds, harmonics, and so on.

At level III and beyond, intensity and viscosity take the place of time. Frameworks IV, V, VI, and VII represent dimensions where vaster relationships of consciousness exist. These concepts become increasingly complex but less specific in scope. They tend to deal more with inter-galactic and inter-Universe relationships than directly with our sphere of action. In each Framework, different metaphors of expression are used to represent the ideas. This requires a different language of interpretation from level to level.

Beyond Framework II, information travels at speeds totally unrecognizable or translatable by us simply because the neuronal connections of the brain cannot function that fast. Spiritually, however, we are able to comprehend and keep up with the rapid flow of information. Consciousness operates at its slowest pace in Framework I, going faster in each level of interaction.

Now back to the evolution of spirit. This Consciousness that we call God existed in its own thoughts in a psychological dimension before mineral, plant, animal, or human entities were created. This infinitely vast Consciousness – the Primary Spiritual Being – can be thought of as having a center of organization and intent. I think of this organizing center as the Supreme Consciousness. It is situated primarily beyond Framework VII. However, this does not imply that the Supreme Consciousness is separate from any part of itself. It is everywhere and everything. It is "All There Is" to use Seth's term. It is in Framework VII that new human entities are formed from the consciousness that comprises the basic matrix of the Universe.

Like human entities, the Supreme Consciousness is involved in a number of various activities – aspects of Being. Each aspect is "managed" by a different facet of the Supreme Consciousness. To a degree, these aspects function almost as if they are separate entities. They are referred to in the Bible as the Seraphim and by other names such as "Watchers" or "Apostles". Nine are responsible for specific activities of the Supreme Consciousness while two others act to integrate and coordinate the functions of the nine. Mankind has been aware of them for ages. Eons ago that aspect dealing with interpersonal relationships was perceived by humans as the God Cupid. The facet charged with overseeing discarnate spiritual entities was believed by the ancient Egyptians to be the God Horus and viewed as a man with the head of a falcon. A third aspect, overseeing all biologic development and reproduction is known as the God Pan. All in all, there are nine general areas of concern and activity with which the Supreme Consciousness deals. As men attempted to perceive them, they presented themselves as these creatures – these visual metaphors. Over time, they were woven into religious stories and became gods of mythology.

Perhaps a better way of understanding this relationship of the Supreme Consciousness to the Watchers is to think of yourself. In this metaphor, assume you are married with a family. In your present state, you are a child as viewed by your parents, a spouse, a parent to your children, an employee to your boss, a friend to your acquaintances, a customer to the supermarket, and so on. In each of these relationships, you present yourself differently and have diverse functions. As a consequence when others view you, each sees you in a different light depending upon your relationship with them. From their singular perspective, you are a different person. If you had a separate body as you performed the various functions, none would encompass the fullness of you, but each would represent you in that particular activity of your total being. Collectively, they are you. Individually, they are not. In like manner, Pan is God, and God is Pan, Cupid, Horus, and all the others, but by themselves, none embody the totality of the Supreme Consciousness.

In the "beginning", the entire Universe with all its parallel and alternate realities were thought-constructions in the mind of the Supreme Consciousness. Stars, quasars, black holes, planets, and asteroids began as ideas, as thought-forms. At the same time, every plant, animal, and human that ever lived, or will live, was/is created in the imagination of that aspect of the Supreme

57

Consciousness known as Pan. Once created, the thoughts-forms began having thoughts, as well. They joined the creative process. From the very first, the entirety of creation was a cooperative venture. Since thoughts are things, existing forever in Framework II, everything and every being was created as a thought-form and simply waited for the ideal time to actualize itself as a physical being.

The individuated creations of minerals, plants, animals, and humans were thought-constructions before they were actualized into this temporal reality. Any appearance in material form is a cooperative venture between The Primary Spiritual Being and the creations themselves.

To express it again, the creation is a continuing process. The physical Universe was not created by a mythical explosion. This is a theory based upon some gross misconceptions and, most important of all, it denies the concept of relative time in which all things exist at once. Indeed, the entire Universe is in a state of unending creation, evolution, and reincarnation at all points of its being from an electron to the largest galaxy and all that exists therein.

The relationship of human spirit to the Primary Spiritual Being could be likened to the development of a corporate structure which began as an idea in the mind of the Chairman of the Board. In the organization, the managers and employees are in a constant state of learning and becoming more deeply involved within the system. As employees gain experience and assume positions of greater responsibility, new ones take their places. Wisdom gained by the employees and managers is taken directly to the Chairman of the Board and is available to everyone. In this manner, the entire corporation becomes wiser. Every employee works at his own pace with help from the managers constantly available upon request. Employees can quit, but no one is fired, and everyone is treated with love and total fairness. It may be helpful to think of the members of the hypothetical corporation as persons cloned in the potential image of the Chairman of the Board.

Unlike a corporation, the Universe contains no actual dividing lines between the various levels of development. The Universe is more like a multidimensional network or matrix wherein specific points of intensity are created with each nidus representing an individuated consciousnesses – a true spiritual syncytium. Medically speaking, a syncytium is a network of cells fused into a continuous mass of protoplasm with many nuclei, all working for the same purpose. The heart muscle is the classic example. The spiritual network of the Universe is constructed in much the same fashion with each entity distinct from the rest, yet not separate; a true paradoxical situation. Keep in mind, this is not the way the Universe is organized. There are flaws and gigantic errors in assuming a corporate structure exists within the Universe, but as a mechanism to aid understanding, this metaphor can be helpful.

In the purest sense, there is no system of power or control as we have been led to believe. This is important, for the minute many people hear terms like "level" or "structure" they get a gleam in their eye and immediately assume that somewhere there is power to be seized. Rather than thinking of levels of development, we should think of vaster organizations of consciousness. However, most religions adopt a concept of an all powerful God controlling the Universe like a hand that controls a puppet. Actually, nothing like that exists within the system – at least not as it is usually presented. Perhaps, the Primary Spiritual Being might be thought of more accurately as an infinitely vast, loving, and attentive Being, rather than a directing and controlling one.

What may be termed "The Supreme Consciousness" of the Universe is undergoing billions of incarnations. This was explained in an earlier chapter, but it bears repeating. Each galaxy is an incarnation of The Supreme Consciousness. This is analogous to our oversouls extending themselves to produce each of our incarnations.

59

The Supreme Consciousness includes all forms of energy which, in their original state, are totally nonaligned. This means that the energy is amorphous, unorganized, and without individuation. The endless supply of intelligent consciousness can be thought of as a reservoir from which individuated entities – galaxies, minerals, plants, animals, and humans – are formed. However, the nonaligned consciousness serves a purpose other than a mere source of "material". In its "non-form" it serves a vital function. It serves as a framework or matrix upon which the aligned beings "play".

Had the Hebrew fathers been more aware of metaphysical concepts and of the nature of the Universe, the book of Genesis might have begun something like this: *"In the beginning, there was intelligent Consciousness, and the Consciousness was God, and God was the Universe. The Consciousness was without form for intent had not shaped it."* This would have set the tone for the Judeo-Christian religion and our society of today in a totally different context. Unless we break away from the belief that God and the Universe are separate, that God created the Universe from without, and that mankind is separate from the Universe, we will be forever caught in a trap of our own making. We will continue to view the Universe as something to be exploited along with the creatures that inhabit it.

As human souls are formed, each develops according to its own potential for growth. Like a snowflake, each is unique and has individual aptitudes and talents for use in its development. In a sense, a human entity acts like a torus, processing energy in much the same way that a black hole and a quasar represent different ends of a cosmic torus and processes cosmic mattergy. Through the action of the internal ego, we acquire information from the vastness of Framework II and integrate it according to our specific purpose and talent. During the procedure, we incorporate the assimilated knowledge unto ourselves and gain wisdom. In this way, we behave like a black hole, pulling in information via our internal ego and its association with

Framework II. Then, through the mechanism of our external ego, the window to our temporal reality and through which we interact with society, we give back to the Universe the wisdom that we gained, modified and shaped by our experience, much as a quasar returns energy to the Universe. Everyone is involved. All creative acts on the part of every spiritual entity become part of the creative act of the Universe.

It is apparent that, at some level, each human being has an opportunity to take part in the creative process. This earthly dimension is our playing field in which each individual, to the degree that it gains wisdom, can participate in the act of creation and participate with the Primary Spiritual Being. It is from the endless supply of nonaligned consciousness that the Primary Spiritual Being creates individuated entities.

Although the core substance of consciousness is the same, there are different *affinities* of consciousness. The various forms of consciousness – mineral, plant, animal, and human – are uniquely endowed with certain, distinct qualities and differ from each other. The nonaligned consciousness from which they are formed might be likened to a deposit of clay. Clay can be dug from the earth and shaped into a brick, pressed into a decorative tile, thrown on a wheel to make a vase, or sculptured into a human figure. While they are created of the same clay originally present in unspecified form, each emerges with diverse characteristics and purposes. Furthermore, a brick is not about to evolve into a tile or a vase into a sculpture. Each final product is distinctive and unique, serving a different purpose and destiny. In rocks, water, and so on – the so-called nonliving things – consciousness exists in a trance-like state, a state of suspended animation.

At the beginning of our journey, through the help of our spiritual guides, each of us were enticed along our selected path of development. This is similar to the way a physicist guides electrons to form particles or waves by the manner in which he chooses to view them. This act of development is endless. A

61

human spirit does not represent an end product. No soul is finished or complete. Each one of us is a work in progress.

As we have said, each spirit is an original designed to follow joyfully the intent of its creator and gain wisdom. Each of us, however, is endowed with the power of free will. As humans, we enjoy more degrees of freedom than do electrons, mountains, trees, and dogs. Limitless avenues of exploration are at our disposal. Consequently, humankind has the potential to create in the same fashion as does The Supreme Consciousness – through its focused intent. This creative potential demands greater attention and responsibility as well.

Keep in mind that mankind is an inseparable part of God, so when mankind creates, God is creating. God is you, and you are God, although you do not encompass the totality of God. This is what is meant by man being created in God's image.

Every creative act, particularly one performed by someone possessing free will, is very fulfilling for the purpose of the Universe. In like manner, if a friend does some thoughtful thing when you gave no hint that you wished to have it done, it means far more than if you had requested it regardless of their willingness to perform the service. Spontaneous, unsolicited gifts are the only true gifts. Many times, the exchange of presents does not involve an act of true giving. The exchange is often one of duty or performed with the expectation of receiving something in return.

In order to make the creation a bit easier to comprehend and to understand how the system works, let us repeat the explanation in a slightly different way. In the beginning, eons ago as we measure time, the Primary Spiritual Being created my individuated entity from the supply of amorphous consciousness in Framework VII. This entity was/is my oversoul or greater-self. Once formed, its potentials were recognized. Accordingly, there were a number of different avenues open to it in its quest for wisdom. While deciding which of these options to exercise, vaster entities nurtured it, enticing its development along various

62

routes of learning. It might have elected to develop in nonphysical planes and never undergo an incarnation. Clearly, this was not the option it chose. It may have chosen to develop only as a biologic form, or it may have selected both avenues of experience. Regardless of the route chosen, its ultimate goal is to gain wisdom and join in the creative process of the Universe.

Since my oversoul chose physical incarnation as one way to learn, it sent splinters of itself into numerous bodies in what can be termed the past, present, and future. Each splinter, with advice from vaster entities, elected to participate in various life scenarios for the purpose of learning and gaining wisdom. One of those splinters is known as O. T. Bonnett. When my lessons are learned, my soul will arrange for its body to die. Upon death of the body, the splinter will return to the oversoul where it will be incorporated into the vastness of that being. In this way, I contribute to the wisdom and knowledge of my oversoul and to the Universe. Upon rejoining the oversoul, the spirit called O. T. Bonnett will retain its individuation despite the fact that it is part of the greater-self.

Should I fail to learn the lesson I selected because of unwise choices, my soul may not be accepted by my greater self. Depending upon the situation, I may reincarnate again and again, facing similar situations, until the challenge is mastered. Only then will my soul be accepted by my oversoul.

Human entities have endless avenues of potential action from which to select their path. They are free to actualize any one or all, for they have "all the time in the world" in which to explore possibilities. In fact, time is an instrument, our brush, with which we work to create our lives much as an artist uses a brush to apply paint to his masterpiece. We must cease thinking of this biologic plane as the only format for learning simply because this is the only one of which we are consciously aware. Physical existence is actually a sort of a side path for attaining one kind of knowledge. There are myriads of other paths from which to choose. Indeed, one is never finished, for the path to wisdom is continuous. As a Tao master would say, "There is no difference between the master and the pupil since they are both on the way. Hopefully, it is a bit more visible when one views the master."

Each human entity is totally unique in terms of what it learns and what it has to offer the Universe. Each of us has complete freedom of choice concerning our thoughts, beliefs, feelings, and behavior. We are free to be stubborn or to behave stupidly. Human consciousness enjoys the power of free will, and the freedom to choose exists throughout the Universe at all levels of being.

I have said that guides and helpers are available to you upon request at every step of the way – providing you ask. Guides are indeed wise, for their experience is far greater than your own. But since they are also human, a guide's knowledge is limited, and they have the potential of making mistakes. They, too, are learning and in the process of gaining knowledge and wisdom. For these reasons, help is not limited to that which can be given by your personal guide. They have assistance from vaster entities when other knowledge is needed.

There is no all powerful entity to which we can turn in times of trouble – at least not in the way we have been taught to think. Since the principle of free will is in effect throughout the Universe, many things are not known until the specific line of probability has been actualized. I am reminded of the story about a venerated seer who was asked if he could foretell the future. He replied that he had no difficulty predicting the future as long as he wasn't asked about something that had not yet happened. Some seers, however, do fairly well predicting the future. Those who are truly gifted have the ability to look at the various probabilities and determine the one most likely to be actualized. Errors come about when the individual involved selects a different probability. So, we see that in human interactions as well as quantum mechanics, the uncertainty principle holds full sway.

Because time is relative and all things are actually taking place at this moment, we are even free to change the "past". Currently, I am participating in a dialogue that triggered a friendship some fifteen hundred years ago as measured by linear time. That relationship produced a dramatic change in history and in our culture – a very awesome and exciting experience. And of course, we are constantly selecting the direction that the future will take. Once we understand relative time and realize that "back then", and "now", and "next year" are happening at once, it all comes clear.

This dimension of the Universe is run by human entities, doing their best to the degree of their capability. Because they have far more experience than we, it runs pretty well. Don't judge the success of the Universe based upon what you observe happening on Earth because our particular line of human consciousness is deeply involved in an experiment of ego empowerment. Keep in mind, that our culture is but one consciousness experiment on one tiny planet in one solar system, and our view is limited beyond belief. So, if something seems to go awry in your life, do not blame your guide, for the chance of a cosmic error is almost out of the question. All things known are available to your guide and through your guide's counselors and in consultation with other vaster, more experienced entities. Despite how your life has turned out thus far, you must acknowledge that you are responsible for it. Through choices of your own, you created it. Your guide is always there to give advice, if you ask. This I know from personal experience.

Many years ago, I was hypnotized by a friend, Jeff Morris, for the purpose of doing some other life recall. I was lying on my living room floor recalling two separate incarnations, the one immediately prior to this when I was a Haitian and the one before that when I was an Apache warrior. Although it was the month of August, it suddenly became so cold in the room that I began to shiver and my teeth chattered so hard that I could barely speak. Later, Jeff said it was cold enough in the room to see his breath.

I felt the hair on the back of my neck rising and heard my voice saying, "I'll be damned, Old Scratch is here!" I had not the slightest idea what I was talking about. Jeff is a seer and able to perceive discarnate entities. He was more than a little upset and asked if I wished to come out of hypnosis. I told him "no", saying that Scratch was an old friend. Again, I had no idea what I meant. I did not even recognize this entity or understand why I thought He was a friend. I only knew that He was in the room, and I sensed that He was standing between the sofa and a chair a few feet from me.

Jeff asked if I could see Him, and at that point, I began to get a mental picture of Scratch. He appeared to be about six feet tall, dressed in a brown robe with the hood thrown back off His head. His black hair was combed back and parted on both sides. Suddenly, I noticed His ears. They were pointed "like Mr. Spock". Between relating my observations about his physical appearance I kept saying, "I'll be damned, Old Scratch is here." Gradually, I became aware that He had hind legs like an ox with cloven hooves.

"He looks like the Devil," I commented, "but I don't detect any hint of evil." Scratch had a wry grin on His face as if He was enjoying a practical joke.

"He's not the Devil," countered Jeff. "He is older than old. He ... He's ... God! Do you notice anything else about Him?"

"Gee, He has little horns!"

"Do you know what horns represent?"

"I have no idea," I answered.

"They stand for infinite wisdom."

It was because of this concept of horns representing infinite wisdom that Michelangelo sculptured Moses with small horns, one on either side of his forehead like I saw on Scratch. The marble sculpture is in Rome, displayed in The Church of St. Peter in Chains.

"But He looks like the Devil," I persisted.

Jeff replied, "O.T. the early church needed a bogeyman to

scare people into doing what the priests wanted them to do, so they used the image of this entity to represent evil. That's why He looks like the Devil. There is no Devil... except in peoples' minds. God encompasses all things. Good and evil are really a paradox. They define one another just as up defines down."

All the time Scratch stood, laughing at me. Later, He informed me that He preferred to be called "Pan". Since then, I found that the joke was on me. I learned that Pan and I are inseparably associated, working together since the "beginning of time", and there I was, behaving as if we had just met. Pan was thoroughly enjoying my confusion. Finally, He turned and walked away, but not before looking back over his shoulder and laughing at me. The room became warmer and my teeth quit chattering. Jeff recorded the session on tape.

Throughout many of my nearly seven hundred incarnations in this dimension I have been involved in spiritual or biologic healing in one way or another regardless of my occupation. Since this is my "last" incarnation, Pan is helping me bring a lot of knowledge and wisdom into focus in this lifetime. For this reason as well as others, He chose to be my spiritual guide in this incarnation. The primary reason for my medical and metaphysical training in this life has been to bring my level of awareness to the point where it was possible to write these books.

Framework II is what Plato was attempting to touch upon when he developed the concept of "ideal forms". Plato maintained that there existed a pure, absolute, conceptual form for everything. Indeed, it is the concept that is real and all else is merely an attempt to emulate the ideal pattern. There is, for instance, an absolute conceptual form of a table, chair, tree, beauty, love, truth, and so on. To use an example, we are all aware of what constitutes the ideal concept of a table. In our present reality, we call certain objects tables in so far as they conform to something that closely resembles the idealized form. If the object strays too far from the ideal, we refuse to recognize it as a table and call it by some other name.

In like manner, in the realm of interpersonal relationships, we hold within our spiritual memory what constitutes true spiritual love. As we interact with others, we recognize certain bits and fragments of spiritual oneness. The more any relationship reminds us of the ideal concept of spiritual love, the more we feel that we are in love with that person.

Years ago, I hypnotized one of my patients for the purpose of doing some psychotherapy. As she came out of hypnosis, she remarked that she wished we had investigated the reason for her intense joy when playing the piano. I re-hypnotized her, and she began moving her hands and fingers as if she was playing.

"Are you a musician?" I asked.

"Oh, yes," she replied with a look of rapture on her face.

"Are you a concert pianist?"

"No, I'm a composer," she countered in a firm voice.

"That's great. What is your name?"

"Tchaikovsky."

"How marvelous!" I responded. "What a wonderful incarnation."

"No. It was a terrible life." She looked very despondent.

"Why?" I asked. "You wrote all that beautiful music. It should have been a very rewarding life."

"That was just the problem. I could never get it right. You see ..." she struggled to find the words, "there is an absolute form of beauty when it comes to music ... and everything else, I guess. My spirit knew this, but I could never get my music to sound the way it was supposed to. I would write and write, each time thinking that I would compose the perfect piece of music ... but I never could."

Poor Tchaikovsky, in his heart, he knew what the ideal form of beauty in music sounded like but did not realize that, because he was attempting to translate it into this temporal dimension, it would not sound the same. It was a goal for which he could only strive and perhaps never achieve except for brief moments in time. My patient confirmed that Plato was correct in his theory concerning the concept of idealized forms. Clearly, objects, definitions, and words are only metaphors, *shadows* of the real things.

Now switch our thoughts to another property of the Universe that I have not as yet touched upon. According to Seth and confirmed by Greg's out-of-body vision and my conversations with Pan, one of the curious things about the Universe is that it pulsates. Every quantum and every atom composing the Universe, all spiritual entities, and all nonaligned energy pulsates. The pulsing is much like a blinking Christmas tree light that is on, then off, and on again. The pulsations are so extremely rapid that from our point of view we appear to be here all the time, much as a moving picture appears to be present at all times rather than rapidly flashing still pictures. As it pulsates, the Universe passes through six other dimensions, disappearing from one and appearing in the next. It spends as much time in each of the other dimensions as it does in this one. They are called parallel pulse dimensions. Therefore, you and I, and the entire Universe are actually "gone" about 86 percent of the time. We have the potential of existing in all of these other dimensions as well. Existences in the parallel pulse dimensions are called probable-selves. In each of the other dimensions, a probable-self is as real as we are in this one. In fact, to each of them, we are a probable-self. In those dimensions, we have the potential of working out other scenarios of possible involvement and action. What might be called the core consciousness of each human entity within any one incarnation is the totality of all seven probable-selves. Due to the "closeness" of these realities, knowledge, experiences, and emotions are frequently exchanged, adding richness and depth to any or all of the lives.

Parallel pulse dimensions are not the alternate realities discussed in previous chapters. The reality into which Greg Satre drove his van where he was surrounded by stars, for example, is a separate dimension from this one in which we live. That alternate reality pulses, too, as consciousness moves through all seven parallel pulse dimensions. Alternate realities, or worlds as some call them, may be structured on an entirely different form of energy such as sound, color, or variations of radiant energy of which we presently know nothing.

Parallel pulse dimensions are superimposed one upon the others, occupying the same space. They are separated only by the fact that each dimension is pulsing in a different time phase from the other six. Thinking back to the discussion of spacetime, this phenomenon is understandable.

Tying all these various layers of energy together in the Earth plane are four main points of energy exchange called coordinate points. In a sense, they are like four powerful "staples" of energy, pathways that join all layers of the Universe together. The points themselves do not have any dimension despite their tremendous energy. They function as channels, exchanging energy and information between all the dimensions. Radiating outward from each main coordinate point, lines of energy connect with outlying regions as well as the Supreme Consciousness of the Universe.

The coordinate points serve a vital function. They intensify psychic intent, enabling tremendous bursts of creative activity to arise and to flourish. It is hardly a mystery why the great civilizations of the past occurred in certain select parts of the world. They evolved where the four coordinate points are located. One is in the region of the Bermuda Triangle where the civilization of Atlantis developed. Another is in the Near East, the so called "cradle of civilization". The third is in the Malaysian Peninsula where many oriental cultures rich in religion, philosophy, and art developed. The fourth is located off the western coast of South America where Lemuria was located. Lemuria, like Atlantis, was a place where early human incarnational experimentation took place. The Galapagos Islands are the tips of mountains that were on the northern portion of Lemuria.

In addition to the four main coordinate points, there are subordinate points that are not as powerful nor as inclusive.

These subordinate points number in the thousands and are created by our individual intent on a "need to have" basis. They do not tie together as many layers as do the main coordinate points, but their function is just as vital on a smaller scale. They are largely responsible for allowing us to solidify mattergy into the stable, material world with which we are familiar. They also act as channels through which we receive information of all types, cosmic and pragmatic. They intensify and stimulate creativity.

I locate subordinate points by changes in air temperature. In my sculpture studio there is one over the stand where I work. I have another small one directly over the dining room table where I do most of my reading. There is a huge one over the chair where I work at my computer, writing and endlessly redrafting my manuscripts as new knowledge is acquired.

Subordinate points also help plants to grow more vigorously and help material things such as buildings to maintain their form and not deteriorate as quickly. They can be described as intensifiers of energy and intent. For instance, a plant's intent is to grow and thrive, and the energy of the subordinate point aids in its purpose. In buildings, the boards, bricks, and girders have intent to conform to the desires of those who built the structures. The subordinate points augment the intent of the materials to comply.

Clearly, the energy forms we call minerals, plants, and animals do not possess the multidimensional possibilities enjoyed by humans. Still, within the more evolved species of animals, there are shadows of developing emotions and relationships similar to those found in human expression, but compared with human consciousness they are rudimentary indeed. However, during loving relationships with humans, animals and plants are able to rise above their normal level of spiritual involvement. This is accomplished by "latching on" to the human consciousnesses with whom they are in close association. Doing so, they experience and participate at levels of awareness not otherwise attainable on their own. This association makes them a bit more than mere dogs, cats, horses, ferns, etc. Through their intimate association with humans, they understand and communicate at higher levels of interaction than an animal or plant of the same species that has no such association. So it is that many pet owners maintain that their pets do things and possess degrees of understanding that scientists insist cannot be so. The pet owners are usually right.

Pets sometimes absorb the negative thoughts and energies of their masters. Doing so prevents their masters from succumbing to illnesses, and the pets may become ill instead. A few years ago, my cat, Barney, performed this service for me. He absorbed the negative energy caused by my outrage at the insanity of the world, and he developed an intestinal tumor. His act of love spared me a serious illness, most likely a colon cancer. Fortunately, I realized what had happened and surgery saved his life. The ability of animals to absorb negative energy explains the healing effects we see in nursing homes and hospitals when plants and animals are brought into those institutions. It also accounts for the calm, soothing experiences I had sitting beneath my Boston fern.

When I was living in Champaign, Illinois I had a lawyer friend and patient who was a nationally known trial attorney. He said that, during a tough trial when he was emotionally exhausted and devoid of ideas and inspiration with which to work, he frequently used plants to rejuvenate himself. He would go outside during the noon recess and find some place around the court house where he could stand on some grass and lean on a tree. He claimed it always helped, and he could return to the court room with renewed vigor and fresh ideas.

He also demonstrated to me an interesting phenomenon in terms of controlling the weather. This is probably as good a place to insert this account as any, for it illustrates the powerful effect that spiritual intent can have upon the cooperative Universe. John and I were visiting one late fall afternoon while walking about his estate. The flower beds were full of blooming plants,

72

and I mentioned that it was a shame to see them killed by the severe frost predicted for that night. He replied that he did not allow the frost to kill his late blooming flowers. I laughed and inquired how he accomplished the feat. At the time, I was just beginning to learn about the workings of the Universe and was both curious and skeptical. He said he did not do it himself, but relied upon "the boys" to do it for him. I expressed total disbelief and jokingly said that I knew he was a bullshit artist but this was going a bit far. He laughed, saying that all good lawyers were BS artists, and added that as a sign, specifically for me, and to prove that "the boys" could do what he claimed, there would be no frost on my property either.

The next morning I arose rather early. The sun was just coming up. I looked out of my upstairs bedroom window and there was the frost just as the weatherman predicted. It was so thick that it looked as if it had snowed. The roofs all about were covered with a thick layer of frost – but there was absolutely none on my garage roof! I dressed and walked outside. The neighbors on all sides had a heavy coat of frost on their property. Their flowers were black and wilted from the freezing cold. Their lawns were covered with frost. However, not one flower or blade of grass in my yard was injured or had one crystal of frost on it. The frost came to the edge of my property line and stopped as if there was an invisible wall of protection which, of course, there was. I called John and told him what had happened and apologized for doubting him. He responded, "Of course, Orvie, I told you the boys would do it." He said he had no frost on his estate either. Wow! What a lesson in cooperative intent!

When scientists make uncompromising statements based upon conclusions drawn from their belief system, they err when stating that animal behavior is due strictly to conditioning, instinct, or genetic programming. They fail to consider the intelligence, creativity, and reasoning capacity of the animals. One example of this assumption in scientific thinking was displayed on a television nature program. The film showed a group of Harris's hawks hunting together. Because of the abundant cover and the relatively small size of the hawk, a single Harris's hawk has little chance of catching a rabbit or any other prey for that matter. The documentary showed a family group of six or seven hawks hunting together. The group split up with some watching from perches in trees or on Saguaro cacti while others got down on the ground and literally chased a rabbit out of the brush into the open. There it was caught with the cooperative effort of several hawks, and they all shared the meal. The commentator claimed the hawks were simply acting on instinct rather than planning the hunt among themselves. He refused to give the hawks credit for logical thinking and planning despite the fact that the hawks did not always play the same role from hunt to hunt. One day, a particular hawk might be in the trees and the next day she might be taking her turn on the ground. In no way, can this behavior be explained on instinct alone.

Underlying all individualized human consciousness is a matrix of human spiritual energy which might be thought of as "common human consciousness" just as there is a common link between trees and between animals. This matrix of common human consciousness joins with the spiritual consciousness of all plants, animals, and the consciousness of the rocks, soil, water, and minerals comprising the Earth. This combined awareness produces a fabric of spiritual energy that forms a platform of cooperative interaction upon which the individualized consciousnesses play. This network of spiritual interaction could be likened to the orchestral music of an opera, creating the background of complimentary musical tones that serve as a framework upon which the human voices can be heard and appreciated.

Recently we have become concerned about the balance of nature. Many are disturbed about the untoward effects that man exerts upon the ecosystems when he takes it upon himself to control nature or exploit it for his own purposes. When man upsets the ecological systems of the Earth, he disrupts the spiritual balance as well. In so far as the spiritual field of play is diminished, man reduces his potential to participate in the creative process of the Universe. As a part of the spirit of God, we must joyfully accept stewardship for that part of the Universe of which we are a part. Since we are part of God, and trees, and wolves, and grizzly bears, and whales, and flies are also part of God, we have an awesome responsibility for every act we undertake. We are charged with this responsibility regardless of how we respond to our obligation. We must be about our primary duty of acquiring wisdom and act upon the knowledge attained through the acquisition of that wisdom with prudence, compassion, and love.

Chapter 4

The Nature of Mattergy

By means of philosophical discussion and information furnished in personal visions and by our guides, Greg and I have determined that the Universe consists exclusively of intelligent consciousness. Moreover, the Universe is an integrated, sentient being – a living entity. For this reason, understanding the mechanism by which information is shared between its various parts is important to comprehending the working of the Universe – and our bodies as well. Beyond that, it is just plain interesting.

Mental telepathy, as telepathy is sometimes called, is one method of communication between plants, animals, and human beings. However, this leads to a problem. Telepathy, as it is ordinarily understood, cannot explain the transfer of information between atoms or between creatures that do not have brains. For this reason, questions immediately come to mind. How does telepathy work? How does information travel from one place to another?

One day Greg called, saying he had a vision in which he was shown the mechanism by which biological creatures receive information at the cellular level. This knowledge bridged an important gap in his understanding certain aspects of the Universe. This question had puzzled him for some time. The vision revealed that in our planetary system the sun is the source and sending station for much of this information. Furthermore, chlorophyll in plants acts as the receiver and translator of the information. All this is more easily understood if we put aside the standard view of the sun as a burning star and think of it as a vast body of intelligent, conscious energy.

To appreciate the importance of Greg's insight, let us digress for a moment. In spite of what we are led to believe, the biologic functions of living creatures are not simply chemical processes that operate automatically, guided by programs contained within the genes. For example, plants require ongoing instruction, concerning which minerals in the soil to take up and in what amounts. They also need constant instruction concerning such things as how to process strange foods and how to handle alien chemicals. These complicated physiologic problems must be addressed and adjusted from moment to moment, depending upon factors outside its control. Not only plants, but every living creature needs information of this sort. Even an authority on cellular metabolism would not know where to begin to tell a cell what to do and how to conduct its life. This does not deny the fact that much of this knowledge is inherent within the consciousness-units and programmed into the genetic code. Regardless, much instruction must be obtained from without in response to metabolic and environmental changes.

We are aware that information exchange takes place between creatures at many levels of being. As previously stated, paired atoms inform each other of the spin of their electrons. Older trees communicate critical information to younger trees. Potato plants warn others of impending attacks by insects. Cleve Backster's philodendron knew when it was being threatened with fire and when the brine shrimp were killed. Backster also demonstrated that he could cause an immediate, predictable response in his philodendron from a distance of many miles by just thinking about it. We know that every cell is in communication with every other cell in the Universe. However, these statements tell us nothing about the method by which this phenomenon occurs. Clearly, Greg's vision concerning the transfer of information was of extreme importance.

Greg went on to explain that a form of "super fast light", traveling at infinite speed, is the vehicle for this information exchange. The energy would have to slow way, way down before it could be perceived as visible light or any other band of radiant energy. His vision indicated that plants receive the instruction directly from the sun and that animals get the information from the plants they eat. All this fits neatly into the concept that the Universe is a cooperative consciousness that exists as a single, integrated, intelligent being.

Wow! Super fast light acting as a messenger! What a concept! The scientific community is still locked into the belief that nothing can travel faster than the speed of light despite some recent evidence to the contrary. Greg and I visited about his vision, but aside from what he had been given, we could come up with nothing else. I was not completely satisfied with the information concerning how animals receive their instruction. No doubt eating plants gives some information, but all animals do not eat plants, not directly anyway. How could the essential data be passed from a plant, to a herbivore or an insect, and on to a predator that eats it, and so on up the food chain?

For me to be comfortable with a piece of information, I must fit it into some logical system of thought and correlate it with other knowledge that I know to be true. One truth does not negate another even when they appear to be in opposition. I always search until I find the underlying message hidden beyond the paradox. To me, Greg's vision seemed incomplete insofar as the way animals received the needed information.

I went to bed that night, asking Pan to give me an answer to the problem while I slept. The next morning I awakened very early. I went to the bathroom, gave my cats some fresh food, and fell back to sleep. I dreamed and, when I awoke, I had a clear understanding of a large portion of the concept. Although still incomplete in many respects, what I was shown appears to be accurate according to Greg and Pan and worthy of passing on even in this rudimentary form.

To digress a moment, I have made mention here and in other places of Greg and I receiving information in dreams, visions, and intuitive flashes. This is not an unusual way to acquire information. Many people who would never consider themselves to be psychic have such experiences. History records numerous examples of people having visions and dreams in which they received inspirations and insights. This sort of experience gives rise to expression, "It came out of the blue." At times, when one has a problem, he will awaken in the morning with the solution. Most people experience such events at one time or another and often "after sleeping on it," respond with, "I just woke up with a great idea!" Usually, this is attributed to integrative thinking accomplished during sleep while the mind is unfocused on other things. While this may be true, more often than not the answer is obtained during an out-of-body visit to another dimension, or a discussion with another entity, or an exchange with a probable-self during the dream state. Since most of us are unaccustomed to thinking in these terms, we explain it in a fashion more acceptable to our conventional belief system.

Early on, physicists made a major error by assuming that nothing can travel faster than the speed of light. The speed of light, or radiant energy, is considered an absolute and a maximum. One exception to this belief came in 1962 when several physicists, while working on solving some of Einstein's equations, came up with the theoretical existence of a subatomic particle that travels at a speed faster than light. This theoretical particle was named a "tachyon". The term is derived from a Greek word meaning swift. To date, there is no proof that such a particle exists, but recent astronomical observations indicate the presence of strange forms of energy that appear to be traveling faster than light. Another exception was mentioned earlier concerning Chiao's work at the University of California in Berkeley. In his laboratory, he discovered photons arriving at a given destination 70 percent faster than light supposedly could have done so. It seems the defended icons of science are starting to topple, at least when it comes to the maximum speed at which things can get from one place to another.

As everyone knows, radiant energy is divided into a number of different bands according to wave length and frequency, ranging from cosmic rays at one end of the spectrum to radio waves at the other. These bands of radiation are simply arbitrary divisions of the total spectrum. It is an established fact that radiant energy travels at the speed of 186,282 miles a second. Now, we are beginning to learn that it was a mistake to consider the speed of radiant energy to be an absolute maximum and declare that nothing can travel faster. Truly, there are no closed loops in science or philosophy. At every extreme lies the seed of the opposite. That is a law of Tao – all things in a dynamic balance with the extremes merely defining one another.

Visible light consists of those wave lengths perceived by the human eye. Other creatures are capable of seeing energy waves that are invisible to us. Bumblebees, for example, are able to see ultraviolet light. Many animals can perceive the energy fields of other animals, enabling them to locate prey in the dark.

Consider that the spectrum of radiant energy extends on either end to infinity. On the long end, the wave length is infinitely long to the point that it is no longer a wave. On the opposite end the wave length becomes shorter and shorter until the energy particles rub together and eventually grind to a complete halt. This can be called matter.

Now, envision a situation in which the Universe floats in a sea of nonaligned consciousness that stretches to infinity in all directions. This nonaligned energy even pervades our bodies and all other structures. Scattered throughout are islands of aligned consciousness representing galaxies, stars, cosmic dust, planets, plants, animals, and humans.

When the nonaligned energy is activated by the sun, one form of energy produced is a burst of activity consisting of cosmic rays, X-ray, light, radio waves, and the others, all mixed up, traveling at 186,282 miles a second. Scientists build instruments and machines that utilize specific bands of this radiant energy. They also learned to produce isolated emissions of specific wave lengths of energy. Thus we have light bulbs that do not emit X-rays, and instruments that produce radio waves without giving off ultraviolet, and so on – at least not at levels that interfere with their primary function.

But as this field of nonspecific consciousness is activated in other ways, waves traveling at *different speeds* are produced, depending upon the manner in which the consciousness is stimulated. When excited in one certain way, a very slow wave is produced in the energy field. These waves travel at 880 feet per second. Due to the slow speed, they agitate air molecules in the atmosphere to oscillate in waves. Our ears pick up this disturbance which we perceive as audible sound. As yet, we are unaware of the energy wave that causes the air molecules to become agitated. Apparently the energy waves of light and those we perceive as sound differ only in the speed with which they travel. Radiant energy travels so fast and the particles are so minuscule compared to the bulk of the air molecules that they hardly produce any disturbance in the air. For this reason, radiant energy does not produce audible sound.

These two bands of energy, one called radiant energy and the other sound, are the only ones of which scientists are aware at this time, but as we will see, they are not the only ones we actually use. Our sensory organs are designed to perceive a narrow portion of each of these two bands. The speed at which energy travels within this total field extends from zero to infinity. This is independent of the wave length. The nonaligned energy is activated by thought and intent as well as the other nonlocal forces. Remember Bell's experiment in which the spinning electrons of the paired atoms exchanged information instantaneously? This occurred, as you recall, regardless of the distance separating them. To my knowledge, physicists have no precise explanation for this instant communication. We submit that this information is transmitted by means of fast-light. Perhaps it is better said that thought stimulates the consciousness field, traveling at infinite speeds to keep all portions of the Universe in communication.

So far, we have considered this process taking place on a flat plane. Once we take into consideration the fact that space is three dimensional, there is another factor to consider and that is one of viscosity or density. Density is based upon the number or amount of energy particles that are placed into motion by a particular stimulus. If we think of the energy wave that travels at 880 feet per second, a few particles will not cause much of a disturbance in the air. The more energy involved the "thicker" the sound wave becomes until it is almost solid. No wonder some prehistoric civilizations were able to cut tunnels through rock by means of concentrating sound with their collective intent. They may have used the short end of the sound wave spectrum which has greater ability to agitate the rock molecules than do the longer waves. Seth explains that the electromagnetic fields formed by thoughts exist physically as sound, but not sound according to the standard definition of sound.

As stated earlier, when energy waves become infinitely shorter they eventually compact into matter. The potential energy contained in matter is phenomenal. In an atomic bomb, less than one tenth of all the potential energy is released. The bomb that destroyed Hiroshima contained a mere two pounds of plutonium. If *all* the energy contained in a few pounds of matter were released in an explosion, it could literally blow the Earth apart – just as the Atlanteans discovered.

When matter is converted to energy through fission, as in a nuclear reaction, a whole gamut of energy forms are released: radiant energy of all wave lengths, slower traveling waves called sound, and everything between, and beyond. Once scientists begin to explore the vast space lying between sound and radiant energy and beyond in all directions they may discover the presence of alternate realities. Instruments can only detect those things for which they were designed, and the designs are limited by the knowledge and imagination of the ones who create them. Einstein has been quoted as saying, "Imagination is everything." He was obviously more than just another scientist with talents for physics and mathematics – he was a visionary.

To return to the original subject, chlorophyll in the leaves and stems of plants acts as the translator of the information received via the fast-light. To some degree, eating plants imparts this knowledge to the animals that consume them, but animals have another mechanism to accomplish this. In man, and many other animals, there is an organ in the brain called the pineal gland. This is often referred to as the "third eye". While physiologists consider its function to be somewhat of a mystery, it is known that there are nerve connections between the pineal gland and the retina of the eyes.

My dream revelation indicated that the pineal gland translates information from the sun for animals just as chlorophyll does for plants. Those creatures not having pineal glands have specialized cells in the eyes or skin that serve the same purpose, responding to fast-light and translating the needed information.

This may partly explain the depression and lack of energy we experience when cloudy weather prevails for extended periods of time. It may well explain why some people are depressed or show abnormal behaviors when they spend most of their waking time during the night hours or work under certain types of artificial light in factories or underground. Our relationship to light needs serious investigation.

The standard, accepted explanation for communication between the brain and the rest of the body is through two mechanisms: hormones produced by the endocrine glands and by the nervous system – the autonomic nervous system, and the cranial nerves. Messages traveling through this elaborate nervous system cause the release of various chemicals, stimulating or sedating certain functions according to specific situations. Endocrine hormones reach the organs and tissues through the blood stream to produce their own effects. This communication system of hormones and nerve stimuli is relatively slow, taking several moments, or more, to produce an effect. On the other hand, transporting information via fast-light is instantaneous.

Water makes up 87 percent of the human body. It is known that water molecules in the body are not haphazardly arranged as they are in a puddle or a lake. Water molecules in the body are aligned to form a gigantic crystal. Some information is transmitted between cells by stimulating the water molecules to vibrate in a specific fashion, instantly carrying information to every cell. It is through these mechanisms, and others, that communication takes place between the external environment and the cells in your body. This is independent of the pineal gland and the nervous system.

Associated with the same system, minute, iron containing, organic salt crystals are present in the nerve cells of the brain. Some years ago when this was first discovered, the popular news media had a field day writing about the "magnets" in the brain, making jokes about their function. Although we do not have the entire answer, we believe that in some way these crystals respond to the coded information received by means of fast-light and are part of the cellular communication system. In addition to this, the iron-containing crystals respond to the energy fields of the various planets thus giving credibility to the field of astrology.

In my book, *Confessions of a Healer*, I spoke of information being delivered to the cells via non-local connections. The example given was that of a person frightened by a near miss from a shotgun blast or a speeding car. The accepted physiologic model is one in which the person sees or hears the alarming event and the endocrine system along with the autonomic nervous system produces physiologic changes that ready the individual to react in an appropriate "fight or flight" manner. Additionally, nerve impulses from the motor cortex of the brain to the skeletal muscles cause the person to react and avoid the danger.

Relying on this time-honored physiologic mechanism to give adequate warning is much too slow. In certain circumstances, to wait for these physiologic responses to trigger a defensive reaction would result in injury or death. In the model I offer, non-local connections instantly warn every cell in the body of the threat. Each cell reacts at once with the appropriate response. A few moments later the nervous system and the endocrine system produce the gross changes of hormone and nerve responses to *support* the cells in their alarm reaction. The mechanism for transfer of the information is in part due to fast-light. In addition to all this, we must bear in mind that the cellular consciousness is precognitive – as is all mattergy. Therefore, the cells know in advance that the gun is about to fire or that the automobile is on its way. Fast-light communication is simply one explanation for the way this response takes place.

Between the speed of zero to infinity a vast number of other dimensions are possible. The various speeds at which energy travels is a continuum rather than sound and radiant energy being isolated, discrete events. Perhaps alternate realities are based upon these various bands of energy. However, to investigate them, we must first believe in the possibility of their existence. While on the subject of the nature of mattergy, let me make one more point about the nature of the parallel pulse dimensions. As previously stated, mattergy was described as oscillating, cutting through seven dimensions of space. Actually, rather than oscillating, it spins as illustrated here.

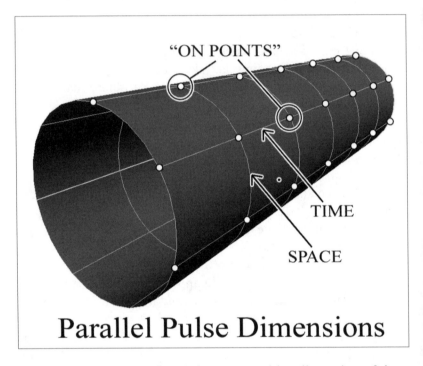

Parallel Pulse Dimensions

As it spins, each time it intersects with a dimension of time, the "spacetime" relationship caused by the intersection of the two factors causes mattergy to "click on" as it were, or pulse, and become manifested in physical form. In the metaphysical sense, a moment and a place are one and the same. An even more interesting model would show the spin of mattergy to bend into a circle, forming a torus. This model might explain other aspects of space and time. Indeed, it may even be a simplified explanation of the string theory that physicists are discussing.

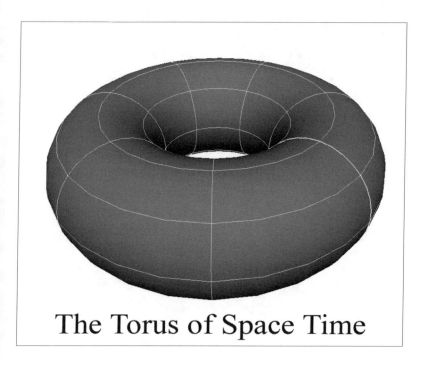

The Torus of Space Time

Much research needs to be done. If we think of energy as a continuum rather than a closed loop or something in isolation, then the horizons of possibility open and new vistas appear. As a species, we need to open our eyes and look at problems and events with our vision unclouded by conventional ideas and prejudice. Something must carry the information we call nonlocal connections. If it is not fast-light, then it appears logical that some other form of communication must exist. It isn't magic or spooky. The Universe is a precognitive, interactive, cooperative, living Being. The existence of fast-light explains many unanswered questions, unravels many an enigma, and opens up a whole new field of research and speculation.

CHAPTER 5

A New View of Evolution

One message I want you to receive is that we must keep our minds open and trust our instincts. We must not allow ourselves to be shackled by conventional wisdom and thinking. This is not to imply that conventional wisdom is necessarily wrong or obsolete. It is only that we should occasionally spend some time in quiet meditation, questioning old beliefs. Indeed, it is far more important to listen to our inner voice than to watch the six o'clock news. The news is always the same. The same things simply happen to different people in different places. So, with an open-minded stance, let us climb upon the fulcrum of the teeter-totter and consider the theory of evolution – how things came into being.

Actually, the concept of evolution embraces not only the development of humans, animals, and plants, but atoms and rocks, as well. Subatomic particles are never considered in discussions of evolution, but to be complete, they must be included if we are to have a meaningful discourse on the subject. Thus, in a broader scope, evolution involves the entire Universe. All things must continually evolve for to remain static or to attain a state of completeness is to insure certain destruction. Indeed, continued existence demands change in one way or another. Furthermore, if these concepts are carried to their conclusion, to deny the principles of multiple incarnations is to deny our own existence.

Before Chevalier de Lamarck and Charles Darwin entered the scene, many theories were offered to account for the profusion of life forms present upon the Earth. Most theories held fast to some form of divine creation. Once created by "the hand of God", animals and plants supposedly changed as a result of pressures applied by nature. The giraffe's long neck was thought to result from stretching to reach the tops of trees and browse on the upper leaves that were more nutritious and contained fewer toxins. According to the theory, the animal with the longest neck had an advantage. Consequently, this trait was gradually passed on to succeeding generations as the short-necked giraffes died off. This conclusion has many obvious flaws. If this reasoning was applied to other examples, then the act of performing appendectomies would eventually result in people being born without an appendix, or operating on people to make their noses smaller would produce humans with little noses at some future time. Indisputably, this will not happen.

Chevalier de Lamarck was one of the first to put forth the premise that all species descended from a single celled creature that arose in the sea. Darwin, in his book *The Origin of the Species*, introduced the theory of natural selection as the final force in determining the ultimate form of a species. His book was published in 1859 and read and discussed by most everyone. Gregor Mendel, a contemporary of Darwin, had not yet published his paper on the inherited traits of garden peas, but it would not have mattered for few paid attention or even heard of Mendel's article published in an obscure journal in 1866. Years later, in 1900, his scientific paper was rediscovered, and Mendel was given credit for his work. Little was known about the function of chromosomes and genes. For this reason, the mechanism by which mutations are produced was not known. When the concepts of genetic inheritance were finally established, they essentially filled the gap in the theory. Mendel's genetics along with Darwin's ideas of natural selection were accepted by the scientific community as the primary, if not the only, explanation for all biologic variation.

A mutation is produced by an error in the duplication of the chromosomes during cell division. This produces an alteration in the physical structure or biologic function of the individual. Mutations can also be produced by damage to genes or by artificial chromosome splicing. The outcome of these events breed true since the change in the genetic structure is duplicated generation after generation – or until another mutation occurs.

Some changes are not due to this mechanism. When a breeder sets out to produce a particular trait in an animal, small size for example, he does not deal with mutations. He takes advantage of the fact that dominant physical traits are inherited. The breeder selects small animals to breed, and the smallest offspring are used for further breeding until the desired size is obtained.

There is another factor at work in breeding programs. To my knowledge, this has never been considered by geneticists. I refer to the cooperative intent of the creatures being bred. Once the goal of the breeder is understood by the plant or animal involved, the spirit of the creature may join in to bring about the desired result. The intent of the breeder entices the animals or plants to alter their own genetic pattern. This is not so difficult an idea to accept. After all, we already know that photons will cooperate in a physics experiment and produce the striped pattern of light and shadow even though they did not pass through any screen. A plant or animal will do no less.

When one considers the multitude of life forms present on the land and in the seas, it is obvious that spontaneous mutations will not account for these variations – at least not alone. Rarely does anyone consider the fact that a spontaneous mutation is as likely to be detrimental to the species as helpful. But mutations are not that common nor does the Darwinian theory of evolution take into consideration that time is relative and that all things happen at once. Considering no factors other than these, it is clear that one form did not give rise to another through endless years of trial and error. Since the old reasoning is faulty, we must abandon the accepted theory of evolution and consider some other explanation to account for the almost infinite number of life forms, both present and past.

Since that aspect of the Supreme Consciousness known as Pan oversees all biologic life, He watches and occasionally stirs the pot of creation gently with His finger. Pan inserts an idea here and there and then sits back, allowing the suggestion to be tried and giving endless opportunity for further experimentation. Thus, we see that the process of change is one of enticement coupled with joyful cooperation rather than an event dictated from without or that of mindless happenstance.

Through its intent, spirit can produce changes in mattergy. We saw this in the experiment in which atomic physicists entice electrons to appear as waves or particles while the electrons, exercising their intent, cooperate with the scientist. We see this demonstrated when a hypnotized individual develops a burn, complete with inflamed tissue and a blister, when he only believes he has been burned. A dramatic illustration of this occurs in people with multiple personality disorders when one personality may be very nearsighted and unable to see clearly without glasses while the other personality has 20/20 vision. Other instances have been reported in which an individual is a severe diabetic and the alternate personality is not diabetic at all. Without question, these examples document that consciousness creates reality – even altering the structure of the physical body or its physiology through desire and intent and often within the span of a few hours.

Lest we render total credit for these effects to the spirit of the individual, it is important to consider the actions of the bio-consciousness, for the cells and the internal ego function in concert. Each cell has its own consciousness which has an affinity with the Earth's consciousness. Cellular consciousness is distinct from that of the mind of the individual albeit closely associated. Every cell is a discrete, living entity which seeks to fulfill its destiny, its desires, its hopes, and its plans. This is done within the constraints of its individuated being and in cooperation with the vaster consciousness of the tissue, and of the organ, and that of the total organism. It is a truly awesome and complex system, and it is helpful for us to know something of this system.

To further appreciate the role of each cell, understand that, in one context, cellular consciousness is a vast complex of memory, containing every isolated moment of experience and perception. The cells hold this vast storehouse of memory at a constant level of awareness ready to infuse these experiences and perceptions – according to our waking, conscious instruction – into the next sequential moment.

Just as we have autonomous physical functions such as heart beat, respiration, and blinking, so do we have autonomous psychological and emotional functions that are partly responsible for the way we structure our perceptual environment. Emotionally, psychologically, or physically, if we hold a certain stance often enough, this stance will become an automatic assumption in our perceptual framework. Furthermore, given the right circumstances, a single event may produce a lasting, powerful effect.

Because the cellular memory bridges all our experiences – experiences that we view in a linear time framework – the cellular memory exists as a "timeless" reservoir of assumptions. These assumptions may be subtly established through childhood events, or introduced through trauma or uncertainty. Groups of similar assumptions may gather in associative blocks, thereby increasing the dynamic of any individual assumption. Often they are not a part of our conscious thoughts and thus become hidden assumptions which persist as conditioned reflexes or appear as illness in other ways.

Clearly, there is much more to our bodies than collections of cells, acting in robotic fashion, following commands from the genes, or as Skinnerian psychologists would lead us to believe, reacting in a purely reflexive manner in response to present stimuli. The cellular consciousness is pervasive, multi-layered, and affects all aspects of our being.

Genes are nothing other than associative energy fields that guide the physical and metabolic energy patterns of the developing creature in specific directions. Genes that "cause" illnesses exert their effects by establishing *tendencies* for certain traits to develop. In addition to these specific functions, at least 95 percent of the DNA molecule and the genes therein serve as off and on switches that modify the action of the other genes. Moreover, genetic tendencies are not indelibly etched into the behavior of cells, thus making the resulting illness, deformity, or trait inevitable. The cells have, stored within, their own sense of purpose and destiny. *The effects of genetic commands are variable because the cells hold differing proclivities and abilities to follow the patterns outlined by the genes. In all cases, the genetic instructions are modified and coupled with the cell's conscious desire to remain healthy and through interaction with the environment itself.* Recently, this has been confirmed and clearly stated by Robert Sapolsky of Stanford University. Overlaying all this are the individual's hidden assumptions and desires that can choose certain genetic patterns or realign them according to its chosen purpose. Hence, if it so wishes, the spirit can negate or augment the genetic program thereby producing or eliminating inherited traits – not by accident or default, but by calculated intention to do so.

The body is constructed in thought-form by the consciousness-units present in the fertilized ovum. At the outset, this thought-form – this electromagnetic field – assumes the energy pattern of the total being even before the fertilized egg starts to grow and divide. The physical body develops along this pattern, further directed by information contained in the genetic code. At this point in its development, the fetus perceives itself to be part of the mother's body, just as do her liver, kidneys, and the other organs.

Once incarnation takes place, the spirit of the infant takes command. Any new directions given by the incoming entity constitute guidelines which the developing body follows. In this way, to some degree or another, you may have designed yourself – at least in part. If you look like your mother and have a dimpled chin or a big nose like your father, it is because you chose to accept the genetic pattern offered rather than utilize your own intent to have a chin and a nose of your own design. I prefer not to think of these intentional changes as mutations although in one sense they actually are. I would rather restrict the term mutation to those accidental genetic alterations that occasionally arise in nature and think of the others as intentional genetic alterations.

To give an example of the above, it is entirely possible for the spirit of the incoming entity to change the sex of the fetus. I know a woman in Michigan who is an excellent psychic and in constant communication with her spirit guide. Acting upon information given by her guide, the woman informed her daughter-in-law that she was pregnant with a male fetus even before the girl suspected that she might be pregnant. Nine months later, the lady was presented, not with a grandson, but with a granddaughter. My friend could not understand the reason for the error since she had received unequivocal information that her grandchild was a male. I suggested that the spirit of the child altered the sex of the fetus.

Her spirit guide confirmed that had been the case. The spirit of the infant chose the family before the woman became pregnant. Then, upon finding the fertilized ovum to be male, the spirit of the yet-to-be-incarnated infant used its intent to alter the genetic code from male to female. When this is accomplished within a few hours of fertilization, it is totally successful. Attempts to alter the sex at a later time usually result in various malformations of the sex organs.

A dramatic example of consciousness creating form was reported in 1998 by some scientists who were studying finches on the Galapagos Islands. The seed-eating species has a strong, heavy bill designed for cracking the tough seeds of the various plants. Because of the increased rainfall produced by the powerful El Niño effect, there was a huge increase in the number of insects on the islands. In response to this, the seed-eating finches launched into a breeding frenzy, hatching seven or eight broods a year! Within a matter of six months – just three or four generations – 70 percent of the seed-eating hatchlings appeared with smaller, more delicate bills that were better designed for eating insects! This event can in no way be explained by the conventional theory of evolution. The alteration of bill structure was accomplished by the intent of the birds themselves to have bills that would fulfill their need in the altered environment.

This feat was accomplished through the action of a number of metaphysical principles working in concert. All consciousness forms – quanta, atoms, cells, plants, animals, and so on – are precognitive. Moreover, they dream of their future. This has been demonstrated in physics experiments in which photons know in advance what the physicist is going to do and cooperate with his intent, producing the desired result without actually going through the experiment. This was mentioned in Chapter I. The finches were precognitive and, in their dreams, the birds envisioned the kind of bill that was needed. They used these dreams to direct their intent and alter the genetic pattern to produce changes in their bill structure. A perfect example of consciousness creating form.

I have stated over and over that consciousness produces form through its intent. It is important to understand that form does not generate a consciousness. Chemicals do not join together to produce compound elements that mysteriously spring to life, nor did life float to Earth from outer space. Neither did apes manage to evolve into men. Human spirit was always human and apes remained apes. But most scientists, caught up in the classic Darwinian theory of evolution, fail to understand this concept.

There is a well accepted theory that over eons of time life evolved in the sea due to constant electrical stimulation by lightening. A well intentioned experiment has been going on for many years, attempting to reproduce this event. The experiment involves the stimulation of a "primordial soup" containing various simple proteins and chemicals with electrical charges in an attempt to produce life. Several years ago, an article appeared in the news announcing a "great development". It seems that some complex protein molecules were discovered in the flask. Stimulating simple protein molecules to combine chemically, however, is a far cry from producing life. In fact, they have nothing to do with one another. But, if Darwin, Sagan, and others who think like them are to be believed, that is what life is – an accident.

During the middle ages, it was thought that lower life forms developed through a process called "spontaneous generation". One of the "proofs" offered for this belief involved leaving a pile of rags and a bit of food in a dark corner only to find mice nesting there at some future time. Since there were no mice in the rags originally, it was thought that in some magical way the mice evolved from the rags. In this modern time, such reasoning is considered ridiculous if not down right silly, but it is no more naive than thinking a collection of chemicals and simple proteins are going to spring to life – with or without electrical stimulation. One wonders if the scientist performing the experiment actually expects to look into the flask some Monday morning only to find a tiny dinosaur walking about or a miniature cave man huddled over a little fire. *Joking aside, it is critical to comprehend and accept that creatures do not develop a property called consciousness nor does matter mysteriously spring to life. Indeed, the opposite is true. Consciousness creates matter and reality. Believing otherwise is no different than accepting the disproved theory of spontaneous generation.*

Keep in mind that all evolutionary changes and developments are taking place at this moment in terms of relative time. All forms of life were/are created at once, period. It is a nice myth to believe that over eons of time one species led to the creation of another through the process of mutation and natural selection, but the truth is that, perhaps with rare exceptions, no such thing happened. *However, because of the unique way in which we perceive time and space, sequential events appear valid in this dimension – and possibly in no other.*

Based upon what has been established, the theory of evolution presented by science is more flawed than that of the creationists who picture God standing outside his creation, molding and forming the creatures of the Universe. Since creation takes place in relative time, all life forms are present at once. Indeed, they always were – and still are. Furthermore, none of the prehistoric plants and animals are actually gone. They did not become extinct. A creature does not cease to exist just because its body dies or it is no longer visible in this plane of reality. These life forms simply do not appear physically on Earth within our narrow view of a linear time and space.

To help comprehend and appreciate the concept of evolution, perhaps it is best to begin at the beginning, remembering that the process takes place in the glorious "at once" of relative time. Evolution began with the simplest kinds of individuated energy patterns. Consciousness-units, being tiny bits of spirit and using their intent and ability to create, followed an idea given to them by The Supreme Consciousness and began playing about. Through their cooperative intent, they created electromagnetic energy patterns called quanta. In their play, quanta joined together, making more complicated fields of mattergy. Some made negatively charged fields while others made positively charged ones. Others had no electrical charge. As they played, eventually a negatively charged energy field began spinning about a positively charged one and the first element, an atom of hydrogen, came into existence. Together, the

98

electron and the proton formed a structure unit. This exploration of consciousness continued as more and more complex relationships were formed. Neutrons joined in the fun and were added to the nucleus along with more positively charged ones. This enticed more electrons to playfully unite in the creative adventure. Utilizing their properties of intent, communication, consciousness, awareness, memory, precognition, and creativity, they combined in wondrous ways. In this manner, other elements were formed through the process we came to call evolution. Electrons, protons, and neutrons continued to explore these avenues of creativity until it became obvious that the larger, more complex atoms were showing a tendency to fall apart, to decay. The atoms realized that this line of experimentation was reaching a dead end.

Then the Supreme Consciousness inserted another idea. What would happen if atoms combined with each other? Taking this idea, atoms launched into an exciting, new course of developmental exploration. This new direction offered a broader opportunity for the creation of involved forms than before. It was great fun. Again, by utilizing their intent and following suggestions of the Supreme Consciousness, molecules and chemical compounds created themselves. This line of evolution was explored to the end. When it became clear that further advances along this path would be of no great value it, too, was abandoned.

At this point, The Supreme Consciousness introduced another concept into the process. The first experimentations succeeded in producing entities that were not biologic in nature. Early experimental combinations of mattergy and spirit resulted in the creation of crystals. Crystals can reproduce themselves. They also have the ability to concentrate or intensify psychic energy by pulling in energy from nearby subordinate points. In some small way, they emulate biologic forms, but in most ways, they are decidedly mineral rather than animal or vegetable.

Then came viruses. They were more like biologic entities. Actually, they are small bits of DNA – the chemical chain which forms chromosomes. Viruses are tiny pieces of bioactive consciousness which are bridges to the plant and animal kingdoms. Viruses cannot reproduce themselves in free form as can crystals, so they dreamed of their future and began to organize other chemicals and proteins to form cells. Some viruses evolved into the more complicated structures we call chromosomes and became an integral part of every living cell. Other viruses remained as such and serve as biochemical messengers. They are responsible for triggering many normal cellular processes and are essential to the continuance of biologic life. On rare occasions, their actions serve to disrupt the physiologic functions of the cells in which they live. When this occurs, viruses are considered agents of disease.

Gradually more complicated forms of plant and animal life emerged. As they played in the fields of the Lord, imposing their intent upon the genetic codes, more and more diversification evolved. At every step of the way, natural selection determined which forms would be most successful in the environment. Whenever Pan, that aspect of the Supreme Consciousness involved with biologic life, deemed that a poke in the ribs was needed to stimulate the process, He did so.

Horses, we are told, evolved from small, five toed animals not resembling a modern horse in any way. As they moved about upon the grassy meadows and planes, a different kind of foot was needed. Whether the original idea for hooves arose from the animal itself, or was suggested by Pan is not important. As horses toyed with the idea of having different feet, they tried out other types in their dreams. By dreaming and using their imagination, perhaps they experimented with webbed ones, or big spongy ones, or some with even more toes than the five with which we think they started. In the environment, natural selection favored the probability that developed the hoof.

Squid, upon contemplating the purpose of tentacles, imagined and investigated in their dreams the serviceability of various lengths. Short tentacles did not prove to be adequate while very long ones were not as efficient as the length upon which they eventually settled. In this manner, the short armed squid and the very long armed squid were replaced by natural selection, or did not choose to manifest themselves in this environment at all. `

All evolutionary changes are contrived in response to specific needs on the part of the creature undergoing the change. We must remember that change is a totally cooperative venture done in collaboration with other creatures and the Universe. Giraffes, in their intent to browse in the tops of trees, responded to the need of the trees to be pruned at the top. Other animals were pruning the sides and the lower branches, but no creature was able to do this to the upper branches. Once the concept of a longer neck became implanted into the mind of the giraffe, the animal took it from there. In a celebration of cooperative adventure, the giraffes imprinted their desire for a longer neck onto their genetic code, and each succeeding generation had a slightly longer neck. This was repeated and refined until the present length was reached and the giraffe was perfectly adapted to his environment. At the same time, the trees' desires and need to be pruned were fulfilled.

It is essential to understand that species do not compete in the way we have been led to believe. Each species cheerfully cooperates with others to produce an environment in which all can exist in a state of cooperative creativity. We are so accustomed to scientists speaking of animals and plants being joined in a life and death struggle of competition that we accept their statements without reservation. *Contrary to what we are told, every species cooperates within the environment for the benefit of all.*

Prey animals do not live in fear of the predators. Remaining alert is not the same as living in fear. I've been in East Africa.

Mostly, the prey and the predators appear to ignore each other. Both understand their role in the cosmic drama. For example, wildebeests supply lions with sustenance while the lions perform a much needed service for the wildebeests – a service they cannot accomplish themselves. By eliminating the old, the sick, the lame, the excess young, and the less attentive, lions prevent suffering, the spread of disease within the herd, help maintain the alertness and the intelligence of the species, and aid in the balance of the ecological system.

When we speak of survival of the fittest, we think of survival being decided on physical terms alone. But, all creatures have a clear understanding that, above all, life is to be enjoyed. The quality of life, not just life itself, is of utmost importance. This is termed "seeking value-fulfillment". In other words, food, water, and shelter often are insufficient by themselves to sustain life. Any individual or species that deems the quality of its life to be below that which allows full appreciation of those values it feels to be essential, simply dies and waits for a more suitable environment in which to return. In some instances, the females kill or abandon their young when they determine that conditions exist in which their offspring will be unable to enjoy life in the way it was meant to be appreciated.

As certain evolutionary experimentations become dead ends, further change comes to a halt. This happens when creatures become perfectly adapted to their environment. As long as the environment remains stable, additional change is unnecessary. The horse's hoof is a perfect example. A hoof is exactly what the horse needs for the terrain on which it lives. Should the environment change, no doubt the horse will change as well, gradually evolving as the situation demands. Other evolutionary dead ends happen when the alteration is not suitable to the environment. These evolutionary forms either discontinue themselves or disappear from our view as seen through the lens of sequential time.

Let us consider yet another look at the creation story. We have talked about the existence of all things in Framework II as thoughts and ideas before they exist in this temporal reality. We have discussed at length the fact that time in the Universe is relative. Now, let us apply these concepts to the act of creation. Remember, our view of the Universe is valid, but very likely it is valid from this perspective and no other. So the mattergy we perceive as rocks, mountains, lakes, and so on may exist as such only in our specific view. This applies equally to the mattergy composing the bodies of plants, animals, and humans. Do not forget that the essential nature of everything is consciousness and has nothing to do with the presence of a material body or form. Therefore, all things – rocks, mountains, rivers, lakes, every species, every subspecies, all variations of life – were/are created as thought-forms in the mind and in the imagination of the Primary Spiritual Being. *And it is/was done all at once.* Strictly speaking, from the perspective of the Universe, there was never a time when rocks, trees, birds, apes, dinosaurs, and humans did not exist. They exist as thought-forms in the consciousness of the Universe – in the mind of God.

As incarnate beings, we tend to focus on physical appearance, forgetting that all things exist as spirits whether they have a material body or not. For this reason, the physical form of any species has nothing to do with the time of its creation, for it always existed. Birds did not evolve from reptiles. Birds always existed. Nor did Homo erectus evolve over time from Ramapithecus. These forms of life always existed and all were created at once in the imagination of the Primary Spiritual Being.

From our position, caught up in the artifice of a sequential time frame, it is very difficult to envision the truth of these statements. Perhaps the greatest deterrent to understanding is that we have been indoctrinated with the Darwinian theory of evolution all our lives and find it difficult to consider any other explanation. Then, too, we stubbornly continue to equate existence with physical appearance. We also remain trapped by the idea that we are biologic creatures that have souls, rather than souls living as biologic creatures – and this is quite a different thing. The emergence of all things in any physical domain is a cooperative adventure on the part of the consciousness of the rocks, water, plants, animals, and humans along with the consciousness of the Primary Spiritual Being. Our linear time construct simply places its own special twist to the story and tends to confuse us.

This concept is so essential to understanding the process of evolution that it should be expressed again. *It is critical to understand that creation of the multiple forms of life – every element, inorganic and organic compound, virus, bacterium, fungus, plant, animal, and human – occurred in one infinitely grand and glorious explosion of creative thoughtfulness. Every creation is, first and foremost, a thought-construction.* Basically, it is immaterial whether any creature becomes manifest in the physical world or not. They exist whether they ever grace the Earth or any other planet for that matter. ***Therefore, the creation of all things is conceptual – not physical.***

Part of our inability to comprehend and accept all this lies in our obsession with physical form. This leads to much confusion and is central to the controversy over cloning. We can clone as many Steven Hawkings, Lance Armstrongs, or Oprah Winfreys as we want, and we will fail to reproduce their souls and their talents. While the clone would be physically identical to the individual from which it was cloned, it would have its own spirit and be a totally different person. In addition to that, the clone would have its own collection of life experiences, all of which contribute to the formation of its personality and skills.

We must cast aside our premature commitment to a view of what the Universe is like and cease limiting our belief to only those parameters that can be documented by our physical senses and instruments, or by science.

We have already said that the Earth is a living being with its own consciousness – a collective consciousness that embraces the consciousness of the air, water, and minerals of which it is composed. These collective spirits of the Earth form a background of energy which nourishes and stabilizes the matrix upon which the plants, animals and humans interact. *Beyond that, consider the Earth as a living entity with physical features that represent creative ventures on the part of the Earth itself as it constantly changes shape and configuration in a cosmic dance of joy. The Earth eternally evolves and reexpresses itself as volcanos erupt and continental plates shift about, rising and falling in an orgasmic display of pure, living exuberance.*

While the Earth is involved with its own creative endeavors, it constantly responds to the emotions, thoughts, desires, and beliefs of the creatures living upon it. Early humans were correct when they believed that they somehow aided in the creation of storms, floods, earthquakes, and other natural events. The Universe is truly a cooperative, living entity and responds to the intent of all. Every part of the Universe is aware when a pebble falls off a cliff or when there is the birth or death of a single being, whether that being is a human or a tiny gnat. Our thoughts actually help create our physical Universe as well as our psychological one.

Today, scientists and others talk of spacetime. This is basic to the theory of general relativity in which time and space are merely alternate expressions of the same dimension. Physicists speak of linear time as real time and relative time as imaginary time. From the metaphysical point of view, they have it backward. Linear time in which things occur in an orderly, sequential fashion is an artificial construction of those who experience it. In any case, some physicists think of relative time as traveling at right angles to linear time. Actually, there are infinite time concepts intersecting our point in space. These divergent "times" help account for alternate realities. Therefore, should you step off onto any one of these other time constructions, you would find yourself in a different space from the one in which you began.

To state the concept in a slightly different way, think of linear time as a path along which we walk. Behind us are memories of events that have occurred and looming in front are probabilities that are yet to be decided upon. Veering off at various angles are other paths representing different time constructions. As previously unseen forms appear on our narrow avenue of linear time, others take diverse forks in the road, ending up in a different space. From their position on the alternate paths of time, they lie outside the restricted view that we hold from our position. They appear to vanish, but they only vanish from our field of perception. For example, if you and a friend are walking down the street and your friend steps into a store to do some shopping, you do not believe that she ceases to exist just because she is lost from sight. So it is with other creatures that no longer exist in our narrowly defined spacetime. Since time and space are in some respects identical, should we travel outside our sequential time line, we would find ourselves in a different space as well. Like unicorns, mermaids, elves, centaurs, dinosaurs, passenger pigeons, and other life forms that no longer appear to be around, they simply occupy another dimension, another place in relative time.

But, since we chose to live in a sequential time construct, I will continue to speak as if linear time and the evolutionary process as we have come to view them are valid and, for purposes of discussion, ignore any other for the moment. As we measure time, it took millions of years for the chunk of earth called India to break away from the east African coast and go slamming northward into the continent of Asia, forcing the abutting land margins upward to form the Himalayan mountains. As the Earth changed with the drift of its continental plates, animals and plants had ample time to adapt to the new conditions. Time, lots of time, is required to make the changes required for survival. (For the moment, forget about the Galapagos finches.) Where man has created such chaos in the ecology, he has done so largely through his ability to alter the environment rapidly.

According to conventional thought, there was one form of placental mammal that split into a number of different branches. One of these gave rise to monkeys and apes. First, gibbons and then orangutans branched off the evolutionary line. Late in the process, gorillas split away leaving a final branch to include both chimpanzees and men. Genetically, mankind is so closely related to chimpanzees that some scientists feel a new phylogenetic classification is needed. They propose that chimpanzees be classified as Homo troglodytes rather than Pan troglodytes. The new classification makes sense. After all, physiologically and physically, we are genetic first cousins.

The final step was taken when human consciousness entered the picture and mankind continued to evolve alone as a totally separate creature. Prehistoric man-like creatures did live in Olduvai Gorge in Kenya and no doubt a lot of other places throughout the world, most of which have yet to be discovered. It is clear that the physical body of humans evolved from the same prehistoric creature that gave rise to all primates – from the same genetic stock as apes – *but human consciousness did not.* So we see that the evolutionists and the creationists are both right and both wrong. Like so many controversies the answer can be found by looking beyond the paradox for the greater truth.

Most of us are familiar with the evolutionary story that has been recounted in scientific articles, books, and television programs concerning man's early, evolutional development in east Africa. According to the anthropologists, the oldest human ancestor was Ramapithecus. This creature evolved some 14 million years ago as we calculate linear time. According to the accepted story, Ramapithecus underwent evolutionary changes over millions of years. Fossil remains seem to indicate that he evolved into Homo erectus about 1.3 million years ago. Scientists say that modern man came into being some 50,000 years ago. Paleontologists make these judgments based upon various physical characteristics. It is obvious that they equate physical structure with humanness and fail to grasp the importance of human spirit as the determinant as to whether a creature was human or not.

The present scientific view is based upon artifacts, tools, and skeletal remains discovered in Olduvai Gorge and other places about the globe. The scenario has been painstakingly pieced together by scientists throughout the world. They have done an excellent job, but their work only traces a single evolutionary line in the development of primates. Regardless of what his physical characteristics may have been, Homo erectus may or may not have been human depending upon whether the creature housed a human soul. I realize I am repeating myself but this is a very important principle to comprehend and accept. We are so blinded by the belief that human consciousness must reside in a body resembling modern man that we miss the point. We fail to concede that it is the presence of a human spirit that defines whether something is human or not. We remain trapped by the idea that man has a soul. *But, mankind does not have a soul. Man is a soul.* A human soul can incarnate into any biological form it desires. A fly, a snake, a wolf, or a tree is human in the purest sense of the term if it has a human consciousness incarnated within it. Clearly, this is an unlikely event for these life forms would be highly restrictive and grossly inadequate vehicles to house a human consciousness. Nevertheless, if a snake had a human spirit, in the purest, technical sense, it would be human.

Let us now consider an alternate explanation of the appearance of mankind on Earth. *According to the best psychic information available, **this** line of human consciousness first came to Earth some 200 million years ago as calculated by linear time.* Prior to their arrival on Earth, they had never undergone a biologic incarnation and, using this criterion alone, could be considered very primitive. They were highly intelligent, and many were extremely advanced psychically, having developed for eons in nonbiologic, spiritual planes. They had no experience handling the challenges of physical existence and the emotional and social problems peculiar to biologic life. These early humans were not stupid. They were just unskilled in the art of biologic living.

These "extraterrestrials" chose isolated valleys and islands on which to begin their incarnational adventures. One location chosen for settlement was a land area west of Peru that folklore now refers to as Lemuria. Here, and at other sites, the newly arrived entities began their search for a physical creature to house them. Generally, they did one of two things. Some drew upon the thought-forms of modern appearing humans and psychically formed their bodies from nonaligned cosmic energy. In this manner, modern appearing men could have been present millions of years before they supposedly evolved.

Others incarnated into the various animal species already present and available. There were not large numbers of these discarnate extraterrestrials in the first place, so they divided into experimental groups consisting of ten or twelve individuals. Each group experimented with a different animal species for the purpose of determining whether those particular creatures were adequate vehicles to house them. Several of the group would enter the creatures and override the animal spirit within. Others would wait until the creature was about to give birth and then incarnate into the unborn animal. In this way, the offspring emerged fully human. If the union showed promise, others joined in the experimental venture. Through their psychic intent they began altering the genetic code to change their bodies into something more suitable just as the Galapagos finches altered their bills. These early unions gave rise to the myths of half-animal half-human creatures, centaurs for example. Recollections of these lives persist in the spiritual memories of some individuals who recall incarnations on Lemuria and elsewhere. These experimental trials were mentioned by Edgar Cayce in some of his psychic readings.

109

Within a 100 million years, as we count time, the fusion of this line of human consciousness with biologic creatures was fairly well perfected. There were primates such as Lemurs in which to incarnate. Lemurs were intelligent with large brains, binocular vision, a useful front foot, and a pelvic structure that could be adapted for more efficient hind-leg walking. This liberated the front feet for more activities. By altering the genetic code of the animals, they created physical alterations quite rapidly. Changes that might never have occurred, or would have required millions of years, waiting for spontaneous mutations, were accomplished in a few generations. In this way, the brain was enlarged, the hand was perfected, and the pelvis tilted to afford an upright stance. Presently, on the island of Madagascar, there is a very large lemur, the size of a small child. Folk lore recounts a time when men and the lemurs were one and lived together. According to the folk tales, mankind finally went away, leaving the lemurs to continue on alone.

Not long ago, I had occasion to hypnotize a young attorney. We were doing some other-life exploration to determine why she was troubled with a severe stabbing pain in her heart. The pain came on when she was under stress or in fear of making an error. She had undergone several expensive medical examinations to determine if the pain was due to a heart ailment, but the tests failed to demonstrate any connection. Through hypnosis, we discovered that the pain was triggered by the memory of a fatal war wound that resulted from an error in battle. Now, any perceived error or fear of making a mistake triggered the stabbing chest pain. Once this was recalled, the pains disappeared.

Then I asked her to recall her first incarnation. She made a peculiar face and shuddered, "I'm all covered with long hair." She went on to describe herself as an ape-like creature about four and a half feet tall, living with a small band of similar creatures. They had no shelter of any kind and at night simply bedded down wherever they happened to be. They had no tools or weapons and subsisted on grubs, insects, small animals, grass seed, fruit, and

110

whatever else they could find as they foraged on the land. They had no spoken language and communicated telepathically. She had no idea where they were, so I gave her a suggestion to project herself high up into the sky so that she could see the topography of the land. She reported that it seemed to be one huge mass of land with no separation into continents that she could determine.

Another individual with whom I had done several hypnotic life explorations was coming out of a trance and remarked that he had a memory-flash of a monkey. I asked him about it. His reply was that it seemed as if he had been the monkey. I rehypnotized him and suggested he recall that particular time.

"Well, it's just a cute, little monkey," he responded.

"What about him?"

"I'm the monkey."

"Don't you mean you're sort of hooking a ride in him? You're not really incarnated as the monkey, are you?" He thought quite a while.

"Yes, I am the monkey."

"What are you doing?"

"Just living in the jungle."

"In what part of the world are you?"

"In Africa."

"Are you able to swing by your tail?"

"Yeah, I could! It was like another hand." He was quite delighted and grinning broadly as he recalled the experience of hanging and swinging by his tail.

"Then you weren't in Africa," I replied. "Only monkeys in the new world have prehensile tails."

"Oh? ... Well, maybe you're right. Africa and South America were awfully close together. In fact, they were touching in some places ... yeah, you're right it was South America. I don't know why I said Africa."

If our knowledge about the shifting of the earth plates is anywhere correct, this account had to be of a period at least 100 million years ago as measured in linear time. Two hundred million years ago the land was still in one massive continent called Pangaea. The Earth's crust began to break apart, forming plates that began shifting about. Fifty million years later, North America had separated from Europe, but Africa and South America were still joined as an expanse of land called Gondwanaland. Gradually, over the millennia this landmass split, and by the late Cretaceous period, some 74 million years ago, the continent of South America had pretty well positioned itself as it is today – or so we think. My friend's incarnational experiment as the monkey was probably about 125 million years ago. But, according to the paeloanthropologists, monkeys did not evolve until 40 million years ago, so in theory, according to the time table we have come to accept, this could not have happened.

Years ago, I hypnotized another one of my patients and did some other-life recall with him. He recounted two lives: one in Medieval Europe, and one in ancient Egypt. The details of his recollections matched with the known facts concerning both of those civilizations. After talking about these two lives for a while, I asked him to recall his very first incarnation. After a moment, he stated that he was not sure whether it was his first or not but he described himself as a cave man. He went on to say that he lived with a group of about twenty-five individuals. I asked what they did. He replied that about all they ever did was hunt, eat, and sleep.

"I was hunting when I got killed," he volunteered.

"What were you hunting? Did a cave bear or lion get you, or was there an accident?"

"We never saw any of those animals. I don't think there were any of them around. No, we were hunting dinosaurs. There was this one kind that wasn't so big and we could surround it and kill it with our spears. They were only about ten or twelve feet high. Boy, they were real stupid."

"What kind of point did your spear have? Was it a flint point?"

"No, we didn't know how to do anything like that." His

112

voice took on an air of pride. "It was a real good spear with a point I made in the fire."

I made spears this way when I was a boy. The end of the shaft was burned in a fire and then the charred wood was rubbed off. Repeating the process and polishing the point on a rock or the sidewalk produced a good, fire-hardened point.

"How did you get killed? Did the dinosaur bite you?"

"No, I was behind him and got too close. He lashed out with his tail and broke my back." This is a killing technique used by crocodiles when hunting on land. The unsuspecting prey avoids the head and forgets about the tail. The crocodile lashes out with its tail, cripples the animal, and then drags it into the water to be eaten.

"What did your friends do when you were injured?"

"They carried me back to our cave. It wasn't all that far. I died a few days later."

I inquired into his thinking ability. After a bit, he said that his thought processes were no different then than they are today. He explained that they had not invented much so life was very simple, involved with the basics of survival. He recalled planning hunts and talking with others about weather, living conditions, making tools and weapons, and things with which they were most concerned. He said their language was very sparse, and as he thought about it, he said most of their communication was telepathic. In fact, he said they had long, involved, telepathic discussions centered about what sounds they would use to designate certain things and ideas.

He went on to say that they carved and molded figures with huge, rotund abdomens. As he recalled this, he began laughing because today it is thought that these artifacts are fertility figures. He explained that they were actually attempts to depict the soul. Scientists often attribute meaning to prehistoric objects and drawings based upon views anchored in modern times.

These early humans were not the stupid, animal-like brutes depicted in movies, books, and television programs. Many would have us believe that prehistoric men were hardly more intelligent than animals and could barely think.

These humans had evolved for eons along discarnate avenues of development. It was only their involvement in biologic life that was new to them. During their previous existence, they communicated very efficiently through the use of telepathy. It was a spoken language they lacked, not intelligence, and while they were developing and refining a vocal language, they continued to communicate telepathically, augmenting this with gestures. This is exactly what animals do. Animals carry on an elaborate telepathic exchange of thoughts and modify this with physical posturing and sounds in much the same way that we use gestures and voice inflections.

In her book, *Mutant Message Down Under*, Dr. Marlo Morgan writes that she thought the Aborigines with whom she was traveling were walking in silence. Later, she learned they were having long, detailed, telepathic conversations. After all, oral language is simply an audible metaphor for mental communication.

But the man I hypnotized gave a perfectly straight forward account of his life as a pre-stone age man using a fire-hardened spear to kill dinosaurs. I had no reason to doubt the accuracy of his other-life recall or that of others I hypnotized over the years. I did not doubt the validity of the lives he recalled as an Egyptian and a European, so why should I doubt he hunted dinosaurs? However, according to conventionally held belief, it could not have happened because man evolved much later, long after dinosaurs became extinct. If valid, his recollection was of an event that occurred more than 60 million years ago. Dinosaurs supposedly became extinct about that time, long before man came on the scene.

But we know better. Several years ago, human footprints were discovered in a sandstone layer dated to be 200,000 years old. Photos of these footprints have been shown in magazines and on television programs. However, what many want to forget and no one speaks about is that near Glen Rose, Texas in the Biloxi river bed, a dozen human footprints were found along side the footprints of a dinosaur in the same layer of sandstone that is dated to be one hundred million years old. Evidence of men and dinosaurs living at the same time does not fit with the defended scientific position. As a consequence, no one is willing to face the issue, and the discovery is ignored.

Not long ago a television program showed drawer after drawer of bones and artifacts that are carefully ignored by the scientific community and stored safely away in a back room of a museum because their presence does not coincide with the accepted scientific beliefs of today.

Other facts and events reported through the years have been overlooked by the scientific community, as well. To name a few examples, knapped arrow heads were found in Mexico in a stratum of the earth dating back 250,000 years. Often mines are sources of ancient artifacts. In a mine shaft near Table Rock, California, miners found ladles, knapped arrow heads and spear points along with mortars and pestles in a layer dated to be 55 million years old. A number of iron balls with inscriptions carved or etched upon them were found in a diamond mine in South Africa at a level dated to be 2.8 billion years old! Even Stonehenge is now thought to be at least 1000 years older than was originally believed.

Incidentally, there has been a renewed interest in cave paintings since some were found recently that antedated by thousands of years the ones we already knew about. Paintings on cave walls were not decorations or made solely for religious purposes. Many of the paintings were maps that told where game could be found, in what numbers, and the direction it migrated. For those privy to the code, the paintings gave all the information needed to make a successful hunt and survive in the area. In the past, other kinds of maps were made using knots on a leather thong or notches carved on a stick indicating distances to travel, river crossings, camp sites, and other pertinent data. All that is required to read any map is knowledge of the code being used.

There is a lot of confusion concerning the time that various things happened. According to conventional knowledge, if humans were present, other mammals had to be present as well. When I asked my patient, who recalled being a cave man hunting dinosaurs, about bears and lions, he said they were not around, so one can conclude they were not in the area or had not yet appeared in his time line. Part of the answer to these confusing accounts is that linear time has undergone some distortional changes which throws our dating methods off. Things we calculate to have occurred thousands or millions of years ago were not nearly that far in the past. If we had some way of calculating time accurately, many mysteries would be unraveled – or others created.

Some time distortions, as related by my hypnosis subject who was incarnated as a monkey long before mankind supposedly evolved, are confusing if we do not consider time as relative. One explanation may be that the "clock" on the linear time bubble might have run backward or stopped and restarted out of sequence. This alone would eliminate huge blocks of "time". Not being concerned with time or when events occurred, perhaps the "clock" did not even exist. Since we have no way to calculate time except as a series of sequential events, this would produce huge miscalculations without our knowing.

Another explanation might be a time warp or a "folding" of time in which things appear to happen out of sequence. In this way, mankind could appear on the scene millions of years before he actually "evolved" – clearly impossible if we consider time only as a linear event. This would be a bit like graduating from high school fifty years before you were born. From the standpoint of relativity such a thing is entirely possible. If we are the observers, witnessing an event from a linear time perspective, these twists in time are impossible to comprehend. If our line of human consciousness did, indeed, arrive on earth 200 million years ago to begin investing its consciousness in various animals, my friend certainly could have been swinging by his tail 125 million years ago. If humans were there, then monkeys could have been there as well.

Still another thing to consider is that other animal forms such as apes, cave bears, or Homo erectus did not have to be present at the time my patient was hunting dinosaurs. As stated previously, small, advanced groups of human consciousness could appear spontaneously and, at will, "borrow" models adapted from the past or future. *The metaphysical is all at once. Sequential, single-direction time functions are specific to reality **agreements** and not limitations to consciousness explorations.* In other words, a person or a group might agree to the linear time concept as it appears to function on this planet, yet have the option to explore other dimensions of time, stepping outside linear time to visit the "future" or the "past". There are also mergers, splits, etc. of probable realities in which developmental progressions of great variation may intersect in any given moment or place. As Einstein taught us through his concept of general relativity, a "moment" and a "place" are much the same.

Regardless of what we think about these time distortions, it is always wise to reflect upon them, exploring probabilities not accepted by the scientific community. Unfortunately, not all scientists are the open-minded scholars that we like to believe them to be. Some oppose new ideas, defending conventional beliefs to the bitter end. In their reluctance to consider new ideas, they often defend traditional beliefs to the exclusion of all else. To my knowledge, only physicists and theoretical mathematicians publish articles containing unconventional, unproven ideas to be read and discussed by the community of their peers. For this, they are applauded. The publication of the new ideas does not guarantee that the concepts are necessarily accepted by the establishment, but they are available to be discussed within the profession.

In his book, *America B.C.*, Fell cites convincing, scientific evidence that regular trade routes existed between Europe and

North America as early as 800 years *before* the birth of Christ. Fell points out that there are far more examples of ancient Celtic writing in North America than in Europe. In Europe, the "pagan" writing was destroyed. In North America, it was not recognized as writing, so it was ignored. Only recently have ancient language experts been asked to look at the markings and scratches found in caves and diggings in North America and contribute their knowledge. They have identified Celtic writing, called "Ogham", as well as ancient Libyan writing and others. In New England, the pilgrims found any number of stone-lined "cellars" which they assumed to be storage rooms. Several of them have Ogham writing carved in the stones, and most are aligned with the summer or winter solstice. The translation of one inscription says, "This is a temple to the God Baal."

Conventional wisdom held to the belief that Europeans did not come to this hemisphere before Columbus arrived in 1492. Long after the remains of a Viking longboat was found in the Great Lakes region and proved to be ancient by carbon dating, some struggled to refute the discovery rather than admit to its authenticity. Ultimately, most scientists modified their belief to accept the fact that the Vikings visited eastern Canada as early as the year 1000 A.D. Fell's book contends that not only the Vikings, but Celts, Libyans, Phoenicians, and others came to North America long before that. Some sailed up the Mississippi river, establishing colonies and trade relations with the Indians 1800 years earlier than did Lief Erickson.

In a cave along the Cimarron River in Texas, there is an inscription written in ancient Libyan stating that the crew of a ship of King "so and so" of Libya took refuge in the cave during a storm. The Zuni language, which is unrelated any other Indian language, is now thought by many to be based upon ancient Libyan mixed with some unknown native tongue – very likely Lumanian. Fell's book gives further examples to support the postulate that Europeans and Africans sailed to the New World more than two thousand years before Columbus landed in the

West Indies.

We need to guard against being trapped by conventional thought. Ideas about ancient times which seem preposterous may be true. One should never fear challenging what is considered an established truth. If belief fails the challenge, then it was a false concept or one aspect of a paradox. Paradoxes are actually windows to greater understanding. The subatomic physicist, Niels Bohr, is reported to have said that no concept can be considered a great truth unless it gives rise to a paradox. Obviously, he was far more than a genius in his chosen field of theoretical and subatomic physics. He was a philosopher of great worth.

The idea that people can recall events that happened ages ago is hard for many to accept. These hypnotically triggered memories of events that happened thousands or even millions of years ago are no more difficult to remember than recalling events of your childhood. Since our oversoul is not involved in sequential time as we are, these recollections are easily brought to mind.

In a long discussion, Ralph and Greg told of another group of human consciousness who came to Earth about 200 thousand years ago. They, like the Lemurians, had evolved in an alternate reality – a nonbiologic plane of existence and came here to experience biologic incarnations. They shifted their "assemblage point", as the author Carlos Castaneda would say, and entered this dimension. They, too, were looking for suitable bodies in which to incarnate. Homo erectus was here waiting for them. What is more, there were as many as fifty varieties from which to choose. Eventually, all but eight or nine were excluded. These may have given rise to the various races that we have today. This group of immigrants may have developed the civilizations mentioned by Seth, as channeled by Jane Roberts. These will be discussed later.

Another group from this same alternate reality entered the Earth plane at a much later date and established the civilization known as Atlantis. Atlantis existed from about 50,000 years ago to about 12,000 years ago. The Atlanteans were quite unique in their behavior. Many chose to keep one foot in Atlantis and the other in the purely spiritual existence in the alternate reality. They would incarnate here and then go out-of-body and return home for a while. For them, Earth was actually the alternate reality. Later on, the Atlanteans quit this practice and remained here. They took their philosophy, knowledge, and technology to other places on Earth namely: Tibet, India, Central and South America, and Nubia which was located where Egypt is today. The question frequently asked by skeptics, "If these things happened, why do we not have archaeological evidence to support the events?" In many cases, we do, but if the artifacts do not fit the presently accepted theories, they tend to be ignored like the human footprints beside the dinosaur tracks in the Biloxi river bed. A better question is, "Why should we have physical evidence of these civilizations?" Actually, to have artifacts or fossil remains of any kind after the span of so many thousands, and sometimes millions, of years and find them is somewhat of a marvel. The reasons for this are several. First of all, there were not that many individuals involved, perhaps a few hundred or at the most a few thousands in small confined areas scattered over the Earth. Then, conditions have to be just right for bones to become fossilized. Furthermore, fossils and artifacts are often hard to spot. In addition, the sites of many of those cultures are now at the bottom of the sea. Possibly more are on land hidden beneath tropical vegetation, waiting to be discovered if only the archaeologists know where to look. One day, archaeologists will make discoveries and document all this to be true. They would be helped greatly by consulting a gifted psychic.

Another civilization established here by a different group was called Lumania. This is not to be confused with the island culture of Lumeria located off the coast of Peru. The primary Lumanian civilization was located in the vicinity of Asia Minor. This, you will recall, is the general location of one of the four major coordinate points in the Earth plane. When the Lumanians came to Earth, their purpose was to develop a completely nonviolent culture. They actually achieved their goal and became a totally passive race. Nonviolence was carried to the point that some individuals fainted or fled from arguments or other confrontations regardless of how minor they were. Unfortunately for them, the nonviolent behavior backfired, rendering them totally incapable of interacting with the other people and creatures in the area.

Placid as they were and unable to survive on the Earth, they isolated themselves by constructing their cities completely underground. According to Seth and confirmed by Greg, this was accomplished, using their psychic abilities. They knew how to focus psychic energy as sound and use it in many ways. Sound was intensified to produce a beam capable of cutting tunnels through solid rock. Using sound, they constructed highly complex cities, complete with living quarters and storage areas under ground. In this way, their inability to deal with violence and discord was solved by staying underground and remaining out of contact with other forms of life.

At least part of their ability to use sound was taught to the Nubians who applied it in the construction of the ancient pyramids found in northern Sudan. These pyramids antedate the ones in Egypt by many thousands of years. Originally, the Nubians occupied the land that is now Egypt. It was the Nubians who carved the sphinx. Later they were displaced by the Egyptians who pushed them upstream along the Nile and deeper into the continent.

The Lumanians constructed underground outposts in various parts of the world. Those outposts reasonably close to major cities were connected by a system of underground tunnels which were cut using sound as a tool. Other outposts were located in the Pyrenees Mountains of Spain, some in Africa, and some in the southwestern part of what is now the United States.

All this seems to be nothing but a tall tale, but some sixty years ago an entire underground city was found in Turkey. I recall reading a short article about the discovery in a news magazine. An opening into the city was found in the back of a cave by a Turkish boy who was playing there, digging around to see what he could find. The city consists of a network of tunnels and rooms carved from solid rock. There are dwelling sites within the city capable of housing several thousand individuals. This underground city was one of the Lumanian communities.

The Hopi Indians of Arizona, as do some other tribes, have a creation myth about their ancestors coming out of an underground world to occupy the land above. This myth is based upon fact as well. The Lumanian people stationed at the outpost in what is now Arizona and New Mexico eventually left their underground city and interbred with the other people in the area to produce a new culture – the people who eventually evolved into the Hopi Indian Nation.

Ultimately, the nonviolent direction of evolution chosen by the Lumanians became completely unsatisfactory. Realizing that their experimental endeavor was impractical and leading to failure, the Lumanians gave it up. Most left to return to their home planet where they originated. Others remained, destroyed their cities, and intermixed with the people in the area. According to Seth, some people living today are incarnational selves of Lumanians and retain their abhorrence of violence in any form, carrying this attitude into present-day incarnations. Often, these are people who faint at the least indication of violence or display other evidence of totally nonviolent behavior.

Greg Satre tells of an incarnation when he was a member of an ancient Nubian culture. While visiting in Egypt, a hostile navy approached intent upon invading the country. Greg and two other Nubians were summoned to stop the attack. The three of them knew how to focus their intent to disperse matter. The energy they used was a form of sound produced by thought. It was the same technique used by the Lumanians to cut tunnels and employed in Nubia to construct pyramids and carve the sphinx. The three of them could use their collective intent to convert matter to energy and create a little, nuclear explosion. The energy from the atoms in a few grams of material has the force of a tiny atomic bomb providing all the energy is released.

Using their talent, they enticed the matter composing the ship's masts to convert to pure energy. This is not unlike the subatomic physicist deciding whether the electron will be a probability wave or a particle. Three of them worked together. One decided which warship to concentrate upon while the other two served to augment and magnify the intent of the first. One by one, several masts burst with a tiny explosion. When destroying masts did not convince them to break off the attack, they completely destroyed three ships. Seeing this, the others turned about and fled, picking up survivors and rowing furiously in an effort to return to their own country. Ancient history tells of several Greeks going down to the shore and setting an entire invasion fleet on fire thus saving their city. The account does not record how they did this, but it may well have been a technique similar to the one Greg used in Egypt.

He recalls a time in Nubia when there were a number of pyramids being built in what is now southern Egypt and northern Sudan. During that period of time, stones were cut using psychic intent as a cutting tool. There were any number of people who had mastered the technique of focusing and controlling sound. A group of fifteen or twenty gifted persons would gather about, cut the stones, and levitate them into place. The process was fairly fast and many of the structures did not take long to construct. Later this technique was used in Egypt in the construction of some buildings during the very earliest periods of the Egyptian culture. I asked why they did not construct all the buildings using this method if it were so efficient. He replied that there were not that many people who had the ability to cut and levitate stones. The ones who could were kept busy. Eventually they died, leaving no one to take their place. Since this level of expertise was no longer available, the Egyptians devised a method of casting limestone blocks in place. This used a large force of unskilled workers and made construction of the huge pyramids possible in a relatively short period of time.

Twenty-five or so years ago, I hypnotized a medical student who recalled a life in ancient Egypt during the time that the pyramids were being built. I asked him how it was done. He thought a moment and then began laughing.

"Hollywood has so little imagination," he said. "No, they did not use thousands of slaves to roll the stone blocks into place. They made the blocks on site. Workers hauled the material up ramps in baskets to the building site and dumped it into wooden forms. Then the priests added a magic liquid that turned it into rock. It only took a short time to make a block, and they made dozens at the same time."

This is almost an exact description of the method of casting limestone cement blocks as given by Dr. Joseph Davidovits and Margie Morris in their book, *The Pyramids: An Enigma Solved*. They give a compelling explanation of how the blocks were cast on site. The magic liquid described by my student friend was water from the Nile River. If one stops to think about it, the idea of dragging stone blocks up ramps of sand and dirt is ludicrous. There is no way logs, weighed down with several tons of rock, could be rolled up a sand or earthen ramp. If you doubt this, ask anyone who has tried to climb a sand dune on foot.

In our enthusiasm over modern technology and what scientists have learned and done, we tend to discount the achievements of older civilizations. We assume that because they are ancient that they were backward and that their level of knowledge and expertise was less advanced than ours. Often they were more advanced especially in the field of psychic skills. Greg tells of a life in which he was a hunter supplying food for a village. There were some in the village who could call him telepathically when his presence was needed. This degree of telepathy was lost as men learned other ways of communicating which did not rely upon individual talent. Not everyone is telepathic to the degree that they can send and receive detailed messages, but anyone can use smoke signals or learn to read and write.

But psychic skills are still preserved by many. Some Tao and Zen masters have the ability to control their energy through focused intent. Some can literally "center" themselves to the degree that they are incapable of being moved even when pushed by someone much stronger and heavier. Karlfried graf von Durkheim told me of a dramatic demonstration by a Zen master that he witnessed while living in Japan in the 1940s. He described the master to be an old man in his eighties, weighing no more than 125 pounds. The master held a bamboo staff between the thumb and forefinger of each hand and challenged anyone to take it from his grasp. He stood, smiling while strong, young men, much larger than he, struggled to wrench the staff from his grip. Not only did they fail, the master did not even appear to struggle as others tugged and pulled in their attempt to remove the staff. Graf von Durkheim said it seemed as if the old man was an iron statue firmly set into concrete. That is unequivocal, focused intent!

A similar feat was shown on the first segment of Bill Moyers' series, *Healing and the Mind*, that aired on PBS television several years ago. It showed an elderly Tao master throwing vigorous, young men fifteen or twenty feet with a tiny push of his hand that sent them flying like rag dolls. Interestingly, Moyers had an opportunity to experience this at a personal level and declined.

But for all their psychic abilities and advanced technology, for one reason or another those early cultures of which I spoke died out, were abandoned, or changed over time. However, some of their ideas and teachings persist in the folklore, myths, and subconscious memories of men today.

Another explanation for the lack of archaeological evidence of many of these cultures is that two of the major ones and many of the smaller experimental ones were island cultures, and most of those islands are now beneath the ocean. If you examine maps showing the under sea topography it is evident that there are huge portions of the Earth's crust that were once above the ocean level and no longer are. Bits of them remain as islands, mountain tops protruding from the ocean. The Galapagos Islands were at one time mountains on the extreme northern part of Lemuria. No wonder there are so many unique creatures found there.

Atlantis was not a single mass of land but a number of large islands and many smaller ones. It was located between Europe and North America. At that time, the continents were closer together. Parts of Atlantis, however, are still above the ocean surface. After the original catastrophe, North America drifted rapidly to the west assuming the general location of today. This continental drift was accomplished within a span of two or three years. The land that did not sink became strung out and is evident today as widely separated islands. Some portions of Atlantis that still remain above the surface of the ocean include: much of the West Indies, Bermuda, the Canary Islands, the Azores, the British Isles, and Iceland. When Atlantis sank, it was not a sudden event except for the original nuclear explosion that triggered the process.

I hypnotized a young man who recalled living on Atlantis. He was in charge of the atomic experiments taking place at the time. He warned the others, working in his laboratory, not to release *all* the energy during their experiments. While he was gone, visiting in Nubia, they apparently failed to heed his warning. When that happened, the explosion vaporized the island on which the laboratory was located, and the huge tidal wave that followed produced wide spread destruction. He said that a fault in the Earth's crust was ruptured and North America began to drift rapidly to the west. The Atlanteans who survived the explosion and tidal wave had two or three years to relocate in other parts of the world before the islands they were living on sank beneath the sea. Some went to Tibet and China while others fled to Nubia,

India, and Central and South America.

Many of the ancient cultures simply left no trace. One reason for this is that their purpose lay in the direction of psychic evolution. These cultures did not concern themselves with the production of durable goods that could survive as artifacts and give evidence of their having existed. When one considers the shifts in the axis of the Earth that have occurred not to mention the shifting of the Earth's plates with land masses sinking and rising, and the changing level of the oceans as ice ages came and went, it would be unreasonable to expect much of anything to be left for us to find.

On at least two occasions huge asteroids struck the Earth, causing the entire crust of the Earth to slip free of the core. The outer layer of the Earth spun rapidly about, moving at least a forth of a turn about the globe, placing the continent of Antarctica at the equator. These slippages occurred very rapidly over a period of a day or two and caused tidal waves that swept across entire continents. An event such as this could account for the presence of coal in Antarctica as well as entire forests of petrified trees in Siberia found lying flat with all the trees having fallen in the same direction.

On other occasions, the fluctuating level of the ocean altered the shape of the continents. One example occurred about 7,500 years ago when the melting polar ice caps raised the ocean level and the Atlantic ocean spilled over into a huge depression filling it. We now call this region the Mediterranean Sea. This, of course, included the Sea of Marmara and placed great pressure on the narrow strip of land that divided the sea from a fresh water lake that was itself in a deep depression. At a later date, heavy rains eroded and softened the land bridge, and the sea broke through at a point we call the Bosporus, flooding the lake, raising the water level about 500 feet, and creating the Black Sea. This gave rise to the Biblical story of the great flood. Recent archeological evidence confirms this natural event.

127

Greg remembers a life in which he lived some 200,000 years ago. Anthropologists probably would have classified him as a Homo erectus. He lived on an extension of land just off the southwest African coast. At high tide, the land bridge separating the higher ground from the mainland was under water, so some of the time the area was an island. It no longer exists above water but lies beneath the ocean and is shown on undersea maps as the Walvis Ridge. He was part of a small community of perhaps thirty people. He says that during his entire lifetime he probably never saw more than five hundred individuals.

He was a hunter, supplying meat for the community and spending a majority of his time away from the village. His only companion and best friend was a huge, black leopard he named Shandar. He and the leopard were able to locate one another by projecting their consciousness into the other's mind and in this way "see" through their eyes. By recognizing the terrain, they knew where the other was and kept in constant touch. Both he and the leopard were able to do this. Greg says that he and his sister in this life were able to do the same thing, and they used this skill in playing games with their brothers and sisters.[1]

He went on to explain that he and the leopard hunted as a team, sharing their kills. They ate what they needed and took the remainder to the village. He states emphatically that his spear was tipped with a flint point.

Several years ago, a friend gave Greg a black cat. From the outset, the cat behaved strangely. Greg would leave the house and, upon returning, the cat would pounce on him from some hiding place and then run off and hide. After a while, the cat would reappear and look at Greg as if to admonish him for not doing what was expected of him.

After a few weeks of these strange goings-on, Greg sat down and meditated about the situation. Once he did, the

---

[1] This skill reminds one of the movie *The Beastmaster*. I asked Greg about this, and he had not seen or heard of the movie.

128

behavior of the cat was obvious. The cat had been Shandar in his previous incarnation on Walvis Ridge. The cat recognized Greg, but Greg had not recognized him as his old friend the black leopard. Greg also recalled a game they used to play. He would go looking for Shandar and the leopard would leap on him from some concealed place and then dash off to hide. Greg would make a big fuss searching for him, and when he found Shandar they would wrestle and play before going on the hunt. Once Greg realized that the black cat was his old friend, he joined in the game of hide-n-seek. What else could he name the cat but Shandar.

It is evident that our present culture is but a chapter in an ongoing cosmic adventure in the evolution of consciousness and all of its material representations. Furthermore, the adventure spans many generations and untold millennia. We are still on the journey.

CHAPTER 6

Multiple Incarnations

Based upon the information already discussed, it is clear that the entire Universe is constantly changing, undergoing evolutionary transformations and, in a very real sense, multiple incarnational existences. We see evidence of this when we look at the billions upon billions of incarnational "siblings" of our galaxy, shining in the night sky. The Universe has no boundaries, and like the Universe, there are no boundaries to the multidimensionality of our existence. It is naive to believe it possible to experience and to learn all that is required from this biological frame of reference in a single lifetime. Limiting our incarnational experience to one life would be like allowing Michelangelo but a single stone to carve or Picasso only one canvass upon which to paint. Therefore, the reality and the necessity of multiple incarnations is rational and inescapable.

Statisticians tell us that more people are living today than the total of all the people who have lived and died since the arrival of human beings on the Earth. Often it is asked, "From where do all the souls come?" Actually, this question has already been answered. The Primary Spiritual Being is constantly forming individuated entities from the nonaligned consciousness that forms the matrix of the Universe. Truly, the supply is limitless. You might compare the process to dipping water from the ocean. In this metaphor, the ocean represents the infinite supply of nonaligned consciousness. Being in endless supply and present at all times, additional bucketfuls are forever available. Another reason for the continuous stream of souls is that human entities are not confined to this planet or to this galaxy. Human entities are free to move about, and do. They can incarnate on any number of planes if they desire, and one entity may enjoy literally hundreds of incarnations throughout hundreds of centuries. Then, we must consider that the statisticians may be at odds with the true facts of the situation. In short, we have no idea how many people lived and died on Earth before the present time.

As indicated previously, the problem most difficult for me to comprehend was the paradox of relative and linear time. If all incarnations are taking place at once in this "eternal now", how could they appear to be happening one after the other? Does not the Earth revolve about the Sun and one revolution take a year? Seasons do not occur at the same time but one after the other. We learn about historical events by studying written records that document the passage of time as history unfolds. Dinosaurs have not roamed the land for millions of years. The great buffalo herds no longer drift unchecked upon the prairie, and the last passenger pigeon died in a zoo in Cincinnati in 1914. Some bristlecone pine trees living today are known to be nearly 5000 years old by actual count of the growth rings. All these things take time. How, then, can it all happen at once? It was a problem for me, but once I understood that linear time is an artificial perception created by the biologic creatures experiencing it, the paradox of relative and linear time became a bit less confusing. Furthermore, everything, every possible event, is present as a probability in Framework II.

One way of comprehending multiple incarnations is to liken each individual life to a portrait drawn on a transparent sheet of paper. Assume that, upon separate sheets, you paint portraits of yourself each representing a single incarnation. Starting with your "first", you might draw a cave man. Then place another sheet on top of the first and paint your second incarnation, perhaps a Celt. On the third, draw yourself as a Chinese woman. Then paint your portrait as the Arab, defending his home from the Crusaders, on another the old Japanese fisherman, and then one as you looked as a Zulu warrior. Continue painting your portraits, stacking sheet upon sheet until you reach your present life. On the final sheet, draw a portrait of yourself as you are today. Depending upon what point in linear time you started your incarnational cycle and how quickly you chose to reincarnate, you may have three, or a dozen, or perhaps several hundred. As you peer at the last portrait, the one of yourself today, because of the transparency of the paper, bits and pieces of all the drawings show through. They are separate portraits representing separate lives, but as you study them, it is apparent that your portrait of today is a composite of all the portraits. For the same reason, your personality today is an aggregate of all your personalities and experiences in your various lives and, of course, the sum total of your experiences in this present life from your birth onward.

When asked who you are, you display the entire stack of portraits which are bound together and compressed into one picture. Your present incarnation represents one extension of your oversoul into this point in history, and the composite portrait represents the totality of the individual incarnations in which your oversoul chose to live. Likewise, your oversoul's experience is a summation of these incarnations plus those of your probable selves and all other involvements and relationships in discarnate and incarnate existences – all of which are taking place this minute. After you complete your incarnational cycle and step out of the linear time sequence, you find there was no first or last incarnation.

Any of the portraits can be placed on top of the stack, and you will appear to others that way. Should you meet someone who knew you in your cave man incarnation you might choose to represent yourself dressed in skins carrying a spear. You create that image in the same manner that you create your present one, by using your intent to appear in that form. A person who knew you as a Scot Highlander might relate to you better if you appeared wearing a kilt and armed with a Claymore. For those who knew you as a German housewife you might be perceived wearing an apron with your hair in a bun. Ralph Warner's spiritual guide uses the name of Hector. He presented himself to Ralph as a Viking warrior complete with a beard, long hair, sword, shield, leggings – the works. That was the way this guide wished to be viewed by Ralph.

A human entity does not necessarily experience a biologic incarnation. Many of the vaster, more evolved spiritual entities, Pan for example, have never undergone a physical incarnation, yet they can be thought of as a kind of human consciousness. Even the Primary Spiritual Being can be thought of as human in a certain limited sense. The Atlanteans and Lumanians had not experienced biological incarnations until they came to the Earth, still they were human before they arrived.

There are endless numbers of nonphysical planes of interaction in which one can learn and gain wisdom. Some choose to develop exclusively in nonbiologic planes. Others select biologic incarnations to the exclusion of all else. Most of us do both. The choice is up to the individual with counsel from wiser and more evolved entities at every step of the way. As stated before, on no occasion is anyone forced to do anything. The mandate is but one – learn and gain wisdom while enjoying life as a physical body.

If a particular entity is not learning, or refuses to do so, it will reach a point when it no longer wishes to continue despite the urging of its spiritual advisors. Like everything else, to stagnate is to die. Some of these entities are simply incorporated into vaster beings, adding whatever wisdom and experience they accumulated to that of the other consciousness. Others may be incorporated into new human consciousnesses as they form. No bit of wisdom, no matter how fragmentary, is ever lost. However, before this is done, they are consulted and agree to have it happen.

From the perspective of an incarnated entity, time is perceived as a linear construction. We see ourselves living and dying, going through a period of time between incarnations, and then entering the next. This is a paradox. Viewed from relative time it is an illusion, but it appears to happen in this manner as long as we are in an incarnational cycle. Within this format, we can take knowledge gained in one life and build upon it in the next. However, transfer of knowledge is not limited to that gained from the "past" because knowledge can be borrowed from "future" lives as well. This is accomplished through precognitive dreaming and by means of the collective memory of our oversouls. Oversouls exist in relative time, and thereby span all structures of time.

One way of envisioning an oversoul is to use an analogy that has been used before and compare it to your hand. Your hand is a separate structure, but not completely separate for it is attached to the wholeness of your body which can be thought of as the Universe – a true paradoxical situation. Your hand is represented in the reality of space and time in a number of different forms. It extends itself into a thumb, fingers, knuckles, palm, back, and so on. Each part is separate and distinct with its own function and purpose, yet each is an integral part of your hand – another paradox. Your finger is your hand, and your hand is your finger, but your finger does not represent the entirety of your hand. When an object is grasped, the various parts have separate sensations and functions. Your thumb does not experience the event in the same way as do the fingers, or knuckles. Each part is involved in the total encounter, yet all experiences are unique. In one sense, your knuckles, fingers, and so on have separate existences.

When an oversoul elects to incarnate, it sends extensions or what might be thought of as splinters of itself into a number of physical bodies in the past, present, and future. Therefore, despite what feels to be true, the other incarnations I recall were not me. O. T. Bonnett was not incarnated as a Hebrew patriarch, a Chinese seer, a Celtic chieftain, an Italian sculptor, or an Apache warrior. Other extensions of my oversoul were incarnated as those individuals. Therefore, when I have "flashbacks" of these lives, or dream of my death as the Apache, or see myself walking up a mountain path surrounded by yellow flowers, I remember these events through the inclusive memory of my oversoul. Because of the close association that each individual has with their oversoul, it is not all that inaccurate to think of having been incarnated in one life after another in an orderly fashion. It certainly feels that way.

When each of us dies, our consciousness with its memories, accumulated wisdom, and personality returns to the oversoul. There it remains as an integral part of the whole. Upon death of our body, we lose nothing. None of our experiences or knowledge is lost. Indeed, we acquire more. We gain all the knowledge, wisdom, and experience of the other extensions of our oversoul while still retaining our individuality.

One way this might be viewed is to think of yourself. In some ways throughout your life, you have been many different people. You were your parents' infant, their little child, the grade school age kid, the high school student, and so on. As you think of these stages of your life, they are gone and, in a sense, the person you were at those times "died" – no longer exists. The individual you are today incorporates all those various "lives" into your present personality. You can recall how you felt, what you did, how you looked, and many other aspects of those "lives" spent in time. In like manner, your oversoul absorbs the experiences of all your incarnations and investments in the various planes of consciousness with which you become involved.

Through Ralph Warner and his guide Hector, I have some knowledge of my father who died in 1981. Ralph informed me that he was reincarnated in 1984 somewhere in Minnesota into a male infant with the name of Charles Blakely. As background information, at one point in time, my father taught manual training in the high school in Alton, Kansas. Dad also had a great love of maps. We subscribed to *The National Geographic*, and Dad loved the maps. He and I spent hours, looking at them together. Years ago I asked Ralph how Dad was getting along. He said he was fine, and then added that Charles completely confounded his parents in two ways. The first was that, from the time he was old enough to get into his father's woodworking shop, he knew how to use the tools without being taught. He knew, for instance, how to adjust a plane. His father was dumbfounded. I told Ralph that Dad once taught manual training and taught me how to use tools. Ralph went on to say that little Charles also knew how to read maps. Neither his mother or father taught him that. Again, I laughed, saying Dad enjoyed maps and had, in fact, passed his love of maps on to me. "Well," Ralph responded, "so much for natural talent."

There is an incarnational phenomenon known as "counterparts". The purpose of this phenomenon is to give a human entity a broader base of knowledge concerning some aspect of society or life than could possibly be attained in a single lifetime. In general, there are three main scenarios in the counterpart phenomenon. One method is for several oversouls who are friends to send splinters of themselves into various parts of the world and direct their efforts toward the investigation of some specific aspect of human endeavor. During sleep states they go out of body and compare notes and ideas. Then, upon the death of their bodies, they get together and pool their experiences and knowledge.

The second way involves a single oversoul. Assume that an entity wishes to investigate some aspect of human endeavor, the educational system in the twenty-first century, for example. An incarnation as a school teacher in Kenya would hardly give a broad view of education in the world. But, if a number of people, scattered throughout the world, were involved in education, a more complete understanding could be attained.

To that end, an oversoul sends an extension of itself into this century. This one extension then splits into several parts, incarnating as males and females in different countries around the world: a grade school teacher in Kenya, a college dean in Kansas, a pre-school teacher in Tokyo, a school principal in Berlin, a high school teacher in Brazil, and the Secretary of the Department of Health, Education, and Welfare in the United States. Following the death of their bodies, they unite and return to the oversoul with a more complete view of worldwide education than could possibly have been achieved with a single incarnation.

The third counterpart event involves probable-selves. Since they are living out other life scenarios, they may well be involved in differing aspects of similar life events. In dreams, or simply through contact via the internal ego, they may share information and contribute to the overall knowledge of all the probable selves.

Probable-selves can sometimes fuse with each other. To give an example, Greg Satre has a great love of literature, and if he had chosen to do so, he would have been an English literature professor. One of his probable selves did become a professor of English literature. Just recently, he died and part of his consciousness fused with Greg's. The professor was interested in psychic phenomenon, but due to his academic position, he felt he could not afford to become involved. By fusing part of his consciousnesses with Greg, the professor is enjoying metaphysics and psychic phenomena by means of this association.

There is another curious aspect of incarnation commonly called a "walk-in". In this situation, another spirit may step into a body as the original one leaves. When an individual elects to vacate a serviceable body, another soul may enter it, take over, and continue on. This is not a common occurrence, but it does happen. Usually, the entity who walks-in wishes to skip the process of birth, infancy, and childhood in order to enter life at a precise moment in time. He or she may have some lesson to give others, and the life situation of the one who checks out affords an excellent opportunity to do so. Other reasons may play a part, as well. Walk-ins simply take advantage of the moment and literally jump probabilities by entering another body. I know one example involving a boy of eleven. He sustained a minor head injury and remained semi-conscious for a week or so. The doctors could find no reason for his long-standing condition. One day, the boy suddenly woke up and was perfectly normal in every way except that there were some odd behavioral changes. Strangely, he was no longer interested in sports and became a scholar. Many of his food likes and dislikes changed dramatically. In some ways, he almost seemed to be a different person, and in fact, he was.

The first boy had achieved his incarnational goal and used the injury as an excuse to exit this plane. When he departed, he left a perfectly good body and brain with all its accumulated knowledge and experience available for someone else. The bio-consciousness continued to attend the body, maintaining its vital functions until another spirit "walked in" and took over. The new individual brought with him all of his own food preferences and his agenda to be a scholar rather than an athlete.

Usually, the entity who walks-in has some connection with the original person. It may be a probable-self, or a close relative that has already died, or another extension from the same oversoul. I knew a woman who failed to accomplished her spiritual purpose by placing herself in an untenable situation. She tried to jump probabilities and alter her stance in life but found it impossible to do so. Needing another avenue of opportunity, she became ill and checked out. This set up a situation for her father, who had died a few years before, to walk-in. He healed her body and is now attending her family while she continues with her spiritual journey, preparing for another incarnation.

When we elect to incarnate, it is done with a lot of planning. Under normal circumstances, a human spirit does not just hop into a fetus. The lessons to be learned and the circumstances which will facilitate the learning process must be decided upon and arranged. Agreements need be made between others with whom they will interact during their life. Prior to the incarnation, the spirit meets with vaster entities who help develop and plan the whole operation, arranging specific circumstances for learning. Together, a plan is created that will lead to a circumstance in which that assignment can best be fulfilled. If, for instance, the entity needs to learn patience, a life plan might be constructed which will be quite boring. Perhaps it will be one that holds forth promises that are never realized. The individual will be forced to wait endlessly for some goal or achievement that is never realized. Another way one might learn patience is to be crippled and forced to depend upon others to do for them.

There may be pivotal events arranged in advance in which the person is required to make a critical decision. If at the age of 20 you are in an accident that renders you a paraplegic, rest assured that you chose the probability, perhaps before you were born. In any case, the injury is an opportunity to address your life and reevaluate your goals. As a disabled person, you have the option of becoming an embittered, complaining invalid or rising above your injury to become a cheerful, mature person, leading a meaningful life and an inspiration to others. One choice leads down one path while the other takes you to a completely different destination in spiritual development. Your "success" in the incarnation is based upon which path is chosen and how your life is conducted once the choice is made. You are never left alone to make these decisions. Help from your guide is always available, providing you ask and if you are wise enough to listen.

On the other hand, should you learn to make wiser, more mature choices at an earlier age and are more attentive, you may not have the accident, or if you do, you will fully recover. So we see that plans are simply just that and subject to change as we proceed through life.

Once your plan is outlined and you have "signed off on the script", so to speak, there comes the selection of parents. By the act of choosing parents, you determine your race, social-economic status, religion, and many other things. You know in advance whether your parents will be supportive or critical, loving or cruel, rich or poor, just or unjust. All these factors affect the ease by which your life plan may be fulfilled.

If you intend to be a physician, helping to relieve illness among the poor and destitute of the world, you probably would not choose to incarnate as a starving infant in Ethiopia. On the other hand, if it is your goal to learn about starvation through the act of starving so that in a succeeding life you will be better equipped to help the starving millions, that may well be the incarnation you select.

At another level of spiritual exchange, while you are choosing your parents, your parents are agreeing to accept you as their child. Therefore, if you are dissatisfied with your race or your parents are abusive, rigid, and unloving, keep in mind that you chose each other in the interactive, spiritual arrangements that take place in Framework II.

I hypnotized one young woman for the purpose of doing some psychotherapy. Some of her problems hinged upon the fact that her parents were not supportive and far too critical. For this reason, she grew up feeling she lacked some essential quality and did not have their love. She saw herself to be inadequate in whatever she attempted. She was, nevertheless, continually trying, raising a family, taking in foster children, and working at various jobs to increase the family income. I asked her to go to the time when she was picking out her mother and father and find out why she chose them. She replied that she did not choose them. I reminded her that everyone has some input into the selection of their parents. She replied, "Oh that. Well, I did pick that family but not because of my parents. I chose it because I wanted to incarnate into the same family as my older sister, Janet. My entire life has been directed toward gaining approval from her." I knew Janet, and she was a fantastic lady. I also knew that Janet would have loved her sister regardless of what she did or the degree of success she attained. My patient was fortunate to have her for a sister.

Sometimes whole families choose to incarnate together in a number of successive lives. Shirley MacLaine tells in one of her books that this is true of her family. In these situations, the members switch roles from life to life thereby gaining experience through different relationships. If this is true of yourself, you might have been your great grandmother in a previous life and married to your mother or father in another. There is nothing incestuous about this relationship. You are an individual human entity and biological connections are of no real importance except for purposes of learning. One woman, during a hypnotic regression, suddenly exclaimed, "That's why I was so close to my grandfather in this life. He was my father in that life in Russia the 1700's." One five year old I know often tells her mother of a time when she was her mother's mother. Entities switch sexes, races, and religions from life to life.

Sometimes I asked my patients to read the book *Life Between Life* by Dr. Joel Whitton and Joe Fisher. The last chapter contains instructions for self-hypnosis, enabling one to recall other lives. Alice read the book and asked if I would hypnotize her to determine if her self-hypnosis experience had been valid. She thought she recalled a life in which both she and her daughter were killed in an explosion. Afterward, she found herself in another dimension, complaining bitterly that it was all a terrible mistake. While talking with Ralph Warner about her, he said she had lived in India and might have been royalty of some kind. He suggested I might want to investigate that incarnation when I worked with her.

Under hypnosis, Alice recalled a life in Oklahoma in the 1930s married to an oil field worker. They were living in a house near the storage tanks. She was sitting at the kitchen table enjoying her coffee and a cigarette with the morning sun on her back just as she enjoys doing in this life. Suddenly, there was an explosion as the storage tanks blew up, killing her and her twelve year old daughter. She insisted that it was totally unfair. I had her go to the time she was planning the incarnation with the "Old

Ones". She recalled being given only forty or so years to work out her life plan. I suggested she ask the Old Ones about her daughter. She reported that the soul of her daughter was "filling in time", waiting for an important incarnation of her own to be worked out. Then I suggested she might have lived in India.

She responded immediately. "Oh, I'm so beautiful," she exclaimed. "I have such beautiful slippers and gowns."

"Who are you?"

"I'm his favorite."

"Who's favorite?" I asked.

"The Maharajah's. I'm his favorite wife."

Alice went on to explain that her two sons became the Maharajah and the first minister after her husband died. She went on and on about what a wonderful mother she had been. In detail, she described the lavish funeral and the pyre of sandalwood and rosewood on which she was cremated. Tears of joy streamed down her face as she related the event. "I deserved this glory," she said, "for having been such a wonderful mother and because my sons were such fine men." Suddenly, she announced that her brother and sister in this life had been her sons in the life in India. She was delighted they were having another incarnation together. I asked if she wanted to come out of hypnosis.

"No," she responded. "I want the one by the sea and the sand."

She recalled a life in Greece, living with her grandparents. They were happy, fishing, gardening, and tending their goats. Many of the goats were pets. "Then," she moaned, "that Turk came, that terrible Turk!" Apparently there was a war and a Turkish soldier killed her grandfather. Then, in her presence, he raped, tortured, and killed her grandmother. Afterward, he slaughtered her pet goats, smearing their blood all over her. I asked if she had been harmed, and she had not. She went on to explain that she spent the remainder of her life dressed in black, living at the church doing penance.

"Why are you doing penance?" I was puzzled.

"Well, if you must know," she said with disgust, "I'm doing penance for what I did to the Turk in the life before this one."

"Oh, you've met before, have you?"

"Oh yes," she sighed with a tone of resignation. "About twenty lifetimes."

It started when they were cave men. She described herself as more animal than human. She said they did not even have a verbal language, communicating by thoughts, grunts, and gestures. They fought over which females they were going to breed. She claimed that they fought or killed each other during every incarnation they had shared. On one occasion, she was a Mexican girl drawing water from the well. He was a bandit and shot her as he rode into the village.

Suddenly, she announced with glee, "Once, I was a knight in Cromwell's army, and I got him right through the chest with my lance."

"Aw, come on Alice," I objected. "He was just another soldier in the thick of a battle. You didn't even know who he was."

"Our spirits knew," she said with finality.

So it went through time. Then she announced that he was her husband in this life! She explained that they had planned this incarnation together with advice from the Old Ones. They had been strongly advised to incarnate together, marry, and get along! She stated that neither of them had loved the other at first. She often wondered what had possessed them to get married. Now she understood that they had responded to some very stern cosmic advice. She vowed that she would make their life compatible, regardless of what it took. The only reason for this incarnation, she said, was to settle their differences.

Any incarnational pattern may be selected that will lead to wisdom. Groups may elect to be born together and die together. Sometimes whole communities choose to reincarnate as a group. Occasionally, citizens of villages destroyed as a result of war may do so. Read ancient and medieval history and you will learn that this is not an uncommon thing for armies to do. The Huns and the Mongols routinely did this if the inhabitants of a town or village resisted and refused to recognize them as their lords. The tribes of Israel slaughtered whole cities as did the Nazis in World War II. The U.S. government attempted to do the same thing to various Indian tribes. At other times, entire villages were wiped out by plagues and disasters.

If a number of people in any of these situations feel strongly that they are compatible and desire another chance to finish their relationships, they can elect to do so by reincarnating together in the same or another community. Some years ago, there was something to this effect in the news. A hypnotist in Idaho discovered a number of people who had lived together in a town in Virginia during the Civil War. Under hypnosis, his clients were able to give accurate information about the community in Virginia. They described specific details of buildings and graveyards despite the fact that none of the residents in the Idaho community had been to Virginia. My guess is that their lives had been so disrupted by the Civil War that they wanted another chance to complete those relationships.

It is possible for a soul to incarnate without a plan, but this is usually a disaster. More often than not, the life is completely disorganized and pointless. However, this is one way to learn that going it alone is not the best way to launch into an incarnation.

Once the life plan is settled upon and parents are selected, the spirit usually does not incarnate until the fetus reaches the last week or so of pregnancy. Rarely does an incarnation take place early in the pregnancy. I have yet to discover anyone who incarnated at the time of conception, however, the soul is free to do so if it wishes. The child that I mentioned in an earlier chapter who altered her sex from male to female did not incarnate at that time. She simply used her intent to alter the genetic code of the fertilized ovum and waited until a later date to incarnate. In any case, early pregnancy is a highly unlikely time to incarnate if for no other reason than one out of every six pregnancies ends in a spontaneous miscarriage. A lot of work and planning goes into setting up an incarnation, and it would be a waste of time and effort, hopping into a fetus or a fertilized ovum that will not survive.

After the parents are selected, the entity usually prefers to hang around, getting to know the mother and father better. Once incarnated, close observation of this type is more difficult. I did hypnotize one person who did not incarnate until three days after the baby was born. The reason for this mix-up was that the individual who planned to incarnate into that particular fetus refused to do so at the last minute. There was a mad, cosmic scramble to find a substitute. The family situation turned out to be close enough to what this person was looking for so he agreed to the plan.

Ralph Warner was teaching parapsychology some years ago at an eastern university. One of his students was pregnant and, during a class hypnosis session, the entity who was going to be her child contacted Ralph through the help of his guide Hector. Using hypnosis, Ralph taught the woman how to communicate with the spirit of her yet-to-be incarnated baby. Throughout the remainder of her pregnancy she would meditate and talk with the spirit of her son. One day, she called Ralph to report that he was now incarnated in her baby. She delivered ten days later. She kept in touch with Ralph and told him of her high level of nonverbal communication with the child.

Once incarnated, the life plans drop into the subconscious and we become involved with living them. This amnesia of sorts is referred to in some cultures as "crossing the river of forgetfulness". Even though you are not consciously aware of your plan, knowledge of it is there and available to you in your dreams, by listening to your conscience, and by paying attention to your inner thoughts.

146

Dreaming is one of the most important activities in which we are involved. In our dreams, we try out various scenarios of life for the purpose of selecting the one that will best fulfill our life's purpose. For the most part, these dreams take place in Framework II. They are experienced in concert with others who will be involved. In addition to this, all sorts of information is received in the form of dreams. On a more or less nightly basis we leave our bodies and travel to other dimensions. This activity occurs during periods of very deep sleep, not during the light REM dream state. Sometimes we meet friends who are also out-of-body or meet extensions of others who have died. Many strange dreams are recollections of actual visitations to our other incarnational selves or to alternate realities in which our oversoul has extended itself. Some dreams are of probable-selves who are undergoing different situations. The information is presented in symbolic form, and the recalled portions usually make little sense from the perspective of our temporal dimension, but spiritually, the messages are completely understood. Certainly not all dreams are of this type, but many are.

As you live out your life, few of the details are preplanned. You create various situations as you go along and attract them to you. Since you are responsible for the circumstances of your life, you are never a victim. There are no mistakes, no accidents, no coincidences, and no one becomes ill or dies who does not agree to do so. You are totally accountable for your being and your life.

Prior to incarnating, or in the process of living, some of us arrange tests for ourselves. Whether planned in advance or created as we go along, what we perceive as troubles and tragedies are simply glorious opportunities we draw to ourselves for the purpose of spiritual growth and learning. We call certain unexpected events "accidents" or "luck" only because we do not understand the workings of Framework II.

Generally, we are unaware that we create these events and pretend not to know what purpose they serve, or that they even

147

serve a purpose. The child born a cripple or mentally retarded knew of the condition before it agreed to incarnate in the fetus and may actually have sought out the situation. Clearly, pity is an inappropriate response to retarded or crippled individuals. We should admire them for accepting the challenge and cheer them in their endeavor, but we should not feel sorry for them. Being handicapped aids them in their undertaking to master whatever lesson they selected.

Essentially, a handicapped child accomplishes two things. First, he or she is involved with their own incarnational lesson. At the same time, the physical impairment serves as a learning opportunity for the parents and others. The lessons that may be learned in this setting are almost limitless. All may be learning patience, compassion, tolerance, how not to suffer – any number of things.

Years ago, when I was struggling to understand the purpose and the justice of incarnational lessons, I hypnotized a young man who related an interesting event. He recalled a life in England as a boy of twelve. He was playing, rolling a hoop down a steep hill and running so hard he could not stop when he came to a crossroad. As a result, he ran beneath the wheels of a huge freight wagon and was crushed to death.

"What a tragedy!" I exclaimed.

"No, it was a good incarnation. I was a good kid."

"But you were only twelve! You had your whole life ahead of you."

"It didn't matter!" he countered. "It was a good incarnation. I had it all together. Besides, in my next life I lived to be eighty-seven."

"But it was a tragedy for your parents," I argued. This was new to me, and I had not come to understand the complicated aspects of multiple incarnations.

"No, it worked out great for them."

"What?" I gasped. I couldn't believe what I was hearing.

"They had never lost a child before, and this was a lesson

148

they needed to learn."

"You mean it was planned?" I was still shocked.

"Not exactly. It was sort of an accident, but I only had about twelve years for that incarnation. If I hadn't been killed that way, something else would have happened. The freight wagon was handy, so that was as good a way as any."

"What was the purpose of your incarnation as this boy?"

"Just to be a good kid and die so my folks would have the opportunity to learn what it was like to lose a son."

Viewed from the perspective of eternity, it made sense. The child came into that particular incarnation knowing that he only had about twelve years. The parents agreed to accept the lesson before they incarnated into their particular lives. My patient said that he went on to an important learning experience of his own in his next life, and the parents had the opportunity of learning how to handle the grief of losing a child. One could not imagine a more perfect plan for personal interaction and instruction.

Not all lessons are ones of tragedy. Most are involved with learning how to handle interpersonal relationships and life situations in general. How to handle power, poverty, wealth, good looks, homeliness, success, greed, prejudice, and failure are all common lessons to be mastered. Some incarnations are for no other purpose than to learn how to have fun and enjoy life. Some are to discover that we must love ourselves as well as others. Despite what we are so often taught, our first allegiance is to ourselves and to gain mastery of our own incarnational challenges. This is not to say that we should ignore others or abuse them in any way. Indeed, the standard of treatment for others is how we regard and treat ourselves – but our purpose must come first.

I had a good friend whose mission in this life was to learn that she was as important and as deserving of her own love and attention as others. She directed this and several other lives toward self-denial and looking to the needs of others in one way or another. She was locked into this pattern of behavior when she developed an illness. All illness is the result of not fulfilling one's greatest spiritual potential, and she clearly was not fulfilling hers by spending another lifetime, denying her own worth. Her illness was a signal to readdress her life situation and change her stance. She could either check out of this incarnation or, if she were ready to honor her own value of being, then the sickness would resolve itself. The inability to see herself as lovable and worthy of her own attention had set the stage for the illness and was blocking her body's recovery. The decision was critical because, if she continued to deny her opportunity to change, there was no point in prolonging this life.

I had not heard from her for years, but one day, I sensed that she was ill and asked Greg to intercede. He went to her in the dream state, extending his consciousness over hundreds of miles to speak with her at length. Following several conversations, she gained insight into the purpose of her incarnation and the reason for her illness. As a result of Greg's intervention and help, she made a valiant effort to develop a totally new footing in her life based upon considering herself first. But, she was too firmly caught up by her old habits to break them easily. As she began to consider her own desires, ceasing automatically to do the bidding of others, her family, friends, and associates pressured her to continue her old habits of servitude. After a serious attempt to restructure her life, she concluded that she was too locked into her old pattern of behavior by the expectations of others. She could see no practical way to jump probabilities and successfully alter her life style. For this reason, she elected to check out and start over in a new life and a new setting. One day, as I sat in my kitchen, I sensed her presence and realized that she had died. Later I spoke to Greg about it. He agreed for on that particular day as he sat reading she suddenly appeared to him. She came with a message of thanks for his help.

My friend's problem brings up another point over which humans have much confusion. I refer to a belief that is prevalent in our culture that to be a good person we are supposed to put others first. Everyone incarnates for a specific purpose and has their own agenda. Their life is their own and not linked to someone else's. This is not to imply that we should go about abusing others or riding rough-shod through life. It is only to remind us that our purpose must supersede all else while treating others with the same love and concern that we hold for ourselves.

Hypnosis, a form of directed meditation, has been used for thousands of years. The East Indians have done much investigation in this area, and their findings shaped their culture. Usually, when we think of reincarnation, our beliefs are influenced by theirs. The Hindu concept is based upon a tenet that we all begin as lower forms of life and through many incarnational cycles gradually work our way up to become human. They also feel that if one does not learn as a human he may be sent back to incarnate into a lower form of life and start over. In addition to this, the Hindu concept of karma calls for personal atonement and retribution in which every cruel or thoughtless act, regardless of its magnitude, must be addressed by experiencing the same thing at a personal level.

My insight does not agree with this concept. When the body dies, the soul of a heartless, cruel person does not automatically rejoin the oversoul. That splinter will reincarnate over and over until the lesson is learned. Once this is accomplished and at least one life is lived in which the individual faces a similar situation and handles it appropriately, the soul is accepted.

Therefore, in the classic sense, there is no punishment or need for atonement regardless of what we do. We are here to learn while treating others with love and kind regard. However, this does not preclude the possibility that the best way to learn may be to experience the effects of one's behavior at a personal level.

While doing other life studies with the aid of hypnosis, many strange, incarnational stories emerge which are just as valid as the more conventional ones we are accustomed to hearing.

Between incarnations human spirits can, as one of my patients phrased it, "hook a ride" in an animal just for fun and education. I am quite certain Hindu hypnotists encountered this phenomenon and assumed it to be part of a normal incarnational cycle. A sojourn as another creature is rarely a true incarnation although under certain specific circumstances it may be. The process usually involves a fragment of the personality extending itself into an animal, a plant, or an object. There it can experience the Universe from a different perspective. I'm sure as a child you wondered what it would be like to be an eagle or a lion. I know I did. Anyone can experience similar temporal existences if they desire.

The first time I encountered this phenomenon, I was working with an acquaintance under hypnosis. As he came out of the trance, he remarked that he had a memory flash of a fox in Georgia. I rehypnotized him and asked that he recall his memory of the fox.

"It's not a fox," he announced. "It's a great big wolf."

"What about the wolf?"

"I'm in him."

"Are you incarnated as the wolf?" I was totally surprised by his statement.

"No, I'm just hooking a ride. After my last incarnation, I didn't want to be a man again for a while. I saw this big wolf and just got in him." He was referring to a former incarnation as a Seminole Indian. The first white man he encountered landed on the beach in a strange looking boat, and he ran down to make friends. The white man pointed a "stick" at him. There was a puff of smoke, and something struck him in the chest, killing him. For this reason, he elected to take himself out of circulation for a time.

"You mean you possessed a wolf?"

"Something like that. I'm just in him."

"What are you doing in the wolf?"

"Just thinking his thoughts and feeling his feelings. I'm just enjoying being in the wolf. He's a real nice wolf."

"Are you in control?"

"No, I'm just riding along, enjoying being in the wolf. I could control him ... if I wanted."

"Did you ever do that?"

"Yeah, I did once when he caught a beautiful deer. It wasn't hurt much and the wolf wasn't very hungry so I made him let it go. I didn't do that again because he was a nice wolf and had to live, too. That's the way he survived, killing deer."

Another man recalled being in a red fox. I asked him what he was doing. He looked startled and replied with total disgust that he was eating a rabbit that had been dead several days. Before I had an opportunity to respond, he said with complete surprise, "Why it's good!" I asked him what his thought processes were like. He recalled lying in the weeds at the edge of a farm, reasoning which of several approaches to the chicken yard would give him the best chance for success. The house and a dog were in plain view, and he had to plan a route that would expose him the least. He said that as soon as he made his decision he forgot about the other routes and concentrated on his mission. He said he never worried or second guessed himself. I asked if he got a chicken and he replied that the dog saw him and began barking so he ran away.

One young man was doing past life recall when he suddenly exclaimed, "My God! I'm a giraffe! I'd forgotten all about that. What a boring, dumb existence, eating leaves all day and then standing around with your legs spread trying to get a drink of water." I asked him how he came to get into a giraffe. He explained that he and another person had been having some very difficult incarnations filled with hardship and danger. They decided they wanted to rest. His friend talked him into getting into the giraffes. They picked them because they looked dumb and placid. He went on to say that they even chose a part of Africa where there were not many lions. He said, "I used to pray for a lion to come along just to liven things up and give us a little

153

bit of excitement."

One day I hypnotized a young man for the purpose of exploring other lives. After recalling two or three, I suggested he go to an earlier one. He was silent for a long time.

"Where are you?" I prompted.

"I'm in a forest."

"What are you doing?"

"I... I'm ... I'm just ... just there," he stammered.

"Are you alone?"

"No."

"Are you a man or a woman?"

"I ... I don't know." He sounded puzzled.

"Are you a boy or a girl?"

"I don't know ... I'm young," he responded with certainty.

"Well, look at yourself. What kind of clothing are you wearing? Try to get a mental picture of yourself." I was getting nowhere with the questions I was asking.

"I'm not wearing any clothes. I ... My God! I'm a plant!"

"What kind of a plant?" I was surprised as could be.

"Just a little plant with red flowers" he said, smiling.

"If you're a plant, there must be others about like you."

"Not that I know of. If there are any others around I'm not aware of them."

"But you said you're not alone."

"I'm not alone. The trees are there."

He went on to explain that he communicated with the trees in a very basic, nonverbal form of information and emotional exchange. Later, he said what was confusing to him was that he could not perceive his body as he expected it to be. He kept trying to picture arms and legs in his mind and suddenly realized they were branches and roots. Subjects under hypnosis rarely volunteer information. They tend to answer questions put to them in a very literal fashion. This accounted for the difficulty I had obtaining a response from him. He was attempting to respond to my questions in the context indicated by the wording of the questions – and the questions were totally inappropriate.   I hypnotized another friend who dearly loves figurines and statues. Her house is full of bric-a-brac with all sorts of little figures. She recalled once getting into a statue and staying there a long time. She received great satisfaction when people gathered about to admire her. She identified so strongly with the statue that any remarks the viewers made about the sculpture were taken as personal compliments.

This same friend also has an aversion to going to the attic of her house where many things are stored.   She is so uncomfortable that it is almost impossible for her to go there to look for some item she might need. She waits for months for my wife to visit and then prevails upon her to accompany her. Upon inquiry into her other incarnations, she recalled living in an attic apartment in Newcastle, England.   The house caught fire, blocking escape by the stairway, and the windows were too small for her to crawl through them to safety. She died of smoke inhalation.

One of the more interesting hypnotic past life investigations I encountered was with another woman. She recalled several lives that were in no way unusual. Then, spontaneously, she began to remember a strange existence. She said she was an Enurian. I asked who the Enurians were, and she said it was more like what they were. She described herself as a sea creature, and the more she talked, the more it sounded as if she had been a mermaid. She described herself as having long hair, human-like arms and breasts, but a body and tail like a porpoise. I asked what she ate. She was confused by the question and replied that she knew she ate but could not remember what. Nor could she recall what her mouth was like. It is possible they were plankton eaters and did not have a mouth she could relate to. Like the man who had been the plant trying to feel his arms and legs, her memory may have been blocked by trying to feel lips, tongue, and teeth that she did not have.

She went on to explain that Enurians had a problem. They were egg laying creatures and there was difficulty with most of their eggs not hatching. Apparently this had not always been so. It was a "recent" development and the species was dying out despite the fact that they had a very long life span of several hundred years – not unlike some tortoises today. She said every six months all the Enurians had to go to a specific place in the Pacific ocean for a conference. I asked what they talked about. She replied that the major subject of discussion was why their eggs did not mature and what could be done about it. She went on to say that the best theory they had was that the temperature of the ocean had changed. Although they tried laying their eggs in different places, it did not help. She said she had not thought much of the temperature theory, but they never solved the mystery and the race eventually became extinct.

I asked her how she died. She was quite disgusted as she recalled that while swimming to one of those mandatory conferences she was killed by an underwater rock slide.

While meditating on the subject of Enurians, Greg informed me that they were only one of many early experiments conducted by the Lemurians in their search for a suitable biologic form in which to incarnate. There were any number of animal/human experimental models that were eventually abandoned in favor of the ape/human combination. It is through recollection of these trial ventures lingering on in the folk lore and psychic memories that accounts for the myths and beliefs in the existence of such creatures.

Quite often, people feel a sudden attraction to another upon first meeting. If the attraction is intense, it is known as love at first sight. I knew one married couple in which the man immediately fell in love with the woman the moment he laid eyes upon her. He was already married, but the attraction was so strong that he divorced his wife and married the woman of his infatuation. The devotion to his present wife was almost an obsession. He was convinced he had been in love with her in a

156

previous life. Both were interested in learning the answer and prevailed upon me to hypnotize them so they might understand the nearly unreasonable allure.

One evening they came to my home. I had little success hypnotizing the woman, but I was able to hypnotize the man. He recalled a life as an officer in the army of Genghis Kahn. Indeed, he did know her in that life. He described her as a sorceress who was attempting to influence his men in ways in which he did not approve. He tried to deal with her, but she would not cease her activities. He hated her. As a captain, he was responsible for the conduct of his men, and she was causing no end of trouble. Finally, in a fit of rage, he ran her through the belly with his sword. He did not kill her quickly for he wanted her to suffer for defying him. Days later, she died a miserable death from peritonitis. When he met her in this life, his spirit recognized her as the woman he had killed so cruelly. Now, he believes it is payback time and that he must spend the remainder of this life trying to atone for his prior act. In truth, his desire to protect was actually a poorly disguised attempt to control her – something he could not accomplish as the Mongol. Their marriage eventually ended in divorce.

The most important thing to remember is that the goal of individual human consciousness is to gain knowledge and wisdom or to teach others while enjoying life. There are no other purposes. There is help at every step of the way if we listen for it. You remember your plan at some level of your psyche. It is there, just beneath the surface of your conscious thoughts. Your guide whispers to you in your inner mind, suggesting what you should or should not do. We must learn to listen to our inner voice. Sometimes, when we seem totally deaf, our guides use other more direct methods to get our attention. Such a situation occurred to me during my medical training. I was about to continue on a path in my professional life that was not according to plan, and I was totally unaware of the significance of my decision. My guide quite literally shook some sense into me.

157

I had completed half of a four year surgical residency program when I was called into active service during the Korean War. The chief of surgery thought enough of me to hold my slot open in the program. It was a great honor to have him do that. In addition, I was assured that upon completion of my residency I would join a vascular surgery group in Chicago headed by Dr. Ormand C. Julian.

About three months before my term of service with the Navy was over, my parents' family doctor suggested I go into practice with him rather than completing my surgical training. For some reason, unbeknown to me at the time, the more I thought about his offer the more I realized this was a possibility I should give serious consideration.

I was stationed at the naval hospital at Camp LeJeune, North Carolina and living on Topsail Island, an hour long drive to the base. I had no radio in the car so I had two hours every day in which to ponder my decision. How could I make the right decision – one which would direct the remainder of my professional life? I wrote out lists of pros and cons concerning both possible courses of action. My soul searching and praying went on several hours a day for over two months. Eventually, I came to the conclusion that with my talent for using my hands, I should continue with my training and be a surgeon, so I put the problem from my mind.

About two weeks before being released from active duty, I was placing a stack of phonograph records on my record changer. For the moment, my mind was blank as I concentrated on setting the records on the spindle. Suddenly, I felt as if someone had seized me by the shoulders and was shaking me violently. I stood stock still, the records still in my hands, and very clearly a voice inside my head said, "Orville, I want you to go into general practice."

I don't call myself "Orville". I don't even like my name. In my internal dialogue, I refer to myself as "Bonnett". I put the records down and began to shake violently. After I quit shaking,

158

I went to the telephone and called the hospital in Chicago. I spoke with the chief of surgery, telling him that I could not return to the residency program – that I had decided to enter general practice. I said that as soon as I was released from the Navy I would go to Chicago and attempt to explain.

Upon arriving in Chicago, I found the chief of surgery still angry, so I spoke with Dr. Julian. He was disappointed but promised that if I ever changed my mind there would be an opening in the residency program for me and a place on his surgery team. Then, I spoke with a urologist on the staff with whom I had developed a real fondness and great rapport. He listened intently while I recounted the entire incident in detail. Then he asked if I was absolutely certain about the validity of the event. I said, "Dr. Vermeulen, I'm more certain this happened exactly the way I related it than I'm sure we're standing here, talking together right now." He looked deep into my eyes with that piercing look he had and said, "Then you don't have any choice, do you?" We both agreed that I did not.

Looking back over forty-four years of medical practice, I know it was the correct thing to do, and that it was my guide, Pan, who shook me and spoke. The point to be learned is that I was about to make a mistake, and Pan made certain it did not happen.

Another example taken from my practice may help you understand how assistance is always available from guides and others at times of need. Other than minor procedures, I was never comfortable doing vaginal surgery and would not have attempted a vaginal hysterectomy. My associate, on the other hand, performed vaginal hysterectomies and pelvic floor repairs very successfully. The event which I will relate hinged upon his performing a vaginal hysterectomy and pelvic floor repair on a young woman. She had delivered four children which resulted in a severe uterine prolapse with stress incontinence. Without doubt, surgery was indicated, and my associate performed the operation. My task had been to assist him and hold retractors.

Another factor relating to the story was that her blood type was O Negative. This blood can be given to anyone in an emergency, but an O Negative person can receive no other kind. Every hospital keeps some on hand for an emergency. We had given the lady two units during surgery. That afternoon an obstetrical emergency used the two remaining units, so the hospital was temporarily out of O Negative blood. We were not aware of this.

At about four o'clock the afternoon of surgery, my associate asked me to call the hospital and inquire how his patient was doing. He had received no call from the hospital as to her condition. I phoned the floor for a report and the nurse said with disgust, "Well, she's been in shock all day. We wondered when you were going to call." I was angry and yelled, "How can we know she's in shock if you don't report to us?" I slammed down the receiver and told my associate what the situation was. He asked me to go to the hospital and start a blood transfusion. Meanwhile, he finished with his patient and contacted the community's leading gynecologist to meet us at the hospital.

When I arrived in the patient's room, it was obvious that she was completely bled out. Her skin color, including her lips, was a sickly, ashen yellow. A quick check revealed there was no hemorrhage outside, it was all internal. Obviously, one of the uterine arteries had slipped free from the ligature and was bleeding inside her abdomen. I could not hear her heart beat nor feel a pulse. There was no blood pressure that could be detected on the manometer. Her abdomen was swollen and taught. I was angry at the situation. Here was a lovely lady with four children all under the age of six, a devoted husband, and she was dying. Furthermore, I knew there was nothing we could do to prevent her death no matter what we tried. I called the laboratory to cross match her for more blood and to bring a couple of units to her room. It was only then that I was told there was no whole blood to give her. The hospital had already checked with Chanute Air Force Base and the hospital in Danville, and they were both out of that type. The nearest Type O Negative blood was in the regional blood bank in Peoria, about a hundred miles away. The weather was terrible. A severe rain storm with very high winds precluded anyone flying to Peoria to get the blood, and there were no busses scheduled that could bring blood in time to save her life.

I prayed silently and forcefully. "God damn it, God! I can't believe you want this woman to die! If you don't want her to die, then you're going to have to do something because we sure as hell can't!"

Instantly, the hair on the back of my neck rose up, and I was covered with goose pimples. I was filled with elation! I knew something marvelous was going to happen, and I was to be allowed to witness it. I was so excited and charged with ecstasy that I could hardly contain myself. Despite her severe shock, the woman was still conscious. I told her and her husband that she was bleeding internally, and that we were going to take her back to the operating room. I promised them both that she would be alright. Her husband, a trial attorney, looked at me and said, "I don't know why I believe you, Dr. Bonnett, but for some reason I do."

My associate and the gynecologist arrived, and the specialist announced that he was going to attempt to locate the bleeding artery by approaching it vaginally in the same manner as the original surgery had been done.

I blurted out, "That's not the way to do it."

The gynecologist whirled about, glared at me, and snarled, "What the hell do you know about it? How many of these have you ever done?" Scorn was dripping from every word. He was board certified and disapproved of general practitioners doing any sort of surgery.

Very calmly I responded, "I've never done this kind of an operation, and I've not even seen one performed, but you'll never get that uterine artery from below."

"What makes you think it's a uterine artery?" he sneered.

As I spoke, I felt more confident and elated, but I carefully controlled my excitement. "It has to be a uterine artery for her to have lost this much blood this fast. It's retracted into the broad ligament and your only chance is to open her belly and approach the artery from above. Besides, even if you get the bleeder from below, you'll tear down her repair in the process of getting to it, and she'll have to undergo another surgery to have her vaginal floor repaired."

He sneered at me again. "Why worry about the repair? We're trying to save her life."

"She is going to make it," I countered.

"Well, may ... maybe ... Maybe you have a point ... about going in from above. I just never heard of anyone doing it that way before," he replied.

The three of us went to the surgery suite to scrub-up for surgery. My associate and the gynecologist were visiting. I was saying nothing, scrubbing away, still wondering what marvelous thing was going to occur. I was still filled with excitement and covered with goose flesh. Unexpectedly, I became aware of someone standing directly behind me. I turned to see who it was – nobody was there! I resumed scrubbing, but the presence did not leave. Twice more I turned, fully expecting to see something, but each time, nothing. We finished scrubbing and went into the operating room. The "presence" took a position across the operating table from me and perhaps five feet back from the table. It seemed as if I was almost able to see it.

In the meantime, the patient still had no discernible pulse or blood pressure, and she was cold as ice to touch. The anesthetist was giving her saline and a blood expander, but what she desperately needed was whole blood to carry oxygen to the tissues. He was administering oxygen to her through the mask and nothing else. The gynecologist, following my advice, opened her abdomen through an incision in her belly. Her tissues were so starved of oxygen that she was numb. She didn't even feel the scalpel as it sliced through the skin. There was so much blood infused into the tissues that the normal anatomy was completely unrecognizable.

"This is impossible!" the gynecologist said in total frustration. "I'm sorry, your lady will die. There's no way I'm going to find a bleeder in this mess. We don't even know which one is bleeding. We might as well sew her up and prevent a death on the operating table." He started to sew up the abdomen.

The entity was still standing on the other side of the operating table where it had been since we entered the room.

Silently, I yelled to the entity. "You have done nothing! You have to make him look again, and show him where to look."

The surgeon was busy sewing up the abdomen. The moment I spoke to the entity, he dropped the needle holder and took a large 10 inch hemostat from the instrument stand. He reached into the depths of her pelvis with the clamp, into all that purple gunk, and bright red blood spurted out of the incision. He snapped the hemostat shut, and the bleeding stopped!

At the same instant, on the other side of the anesthetic screen where it was impossible for him to see what was taking place in the operative field, the anesthetist said, "Hey, what did you guys do? Suddenly, I can get her pulse and blood pressure."

The surgeon stammered, "I ... I don't know. I guess ... I guess I got a bleeder. What are the readings?"

"Everything is normal! Her pulse is a nice, steady 76 and her pressure is 124 over 72. I can't understand it! I haven't been able to get any pulse or blood pressure since she got into the room."

The entity disappeared.

The surgeon proceeded to close the abdomen with the clamp sticking out of the wound. Three days later he removed the clamp. The lady left the hospital seven days after her hysterectomy.

While we were struggling in the operating room, a friend of the family who owned an airplane volunteered to fly to Peoria to

163

get blood. As I said, the weather was terrible with rain and a terribly high wind, and the airport was closed. He informed the controller at the airport about the emergency and took off against advice. His small plane had an air speed of about 125 miles an hour. Peoria was 100 miles away. He figured, considering the bad weather and high winds, it would take at least three hours to make the round trip. As he took off from Champaign, instead of the 80 mile an hour head wind he'd been told to expect, he caught a terrific tail wind and arrived in Peoria in a little less than thirty minutes. The blood was waiting at the airport. They put it on the plane and he took off. He expected to fight the wind that had whisked him to Peoria as he flew back to Champaign, but instead caught another tail wind! He landed in Champaign with the round trip taking a bit over an hour. Eight pints of blood were waiting as we wheeled the lady from the operating room.

Except for suggesting that the surgeon use an abdominal approach, I was not involved in the incident other than being aware of what was happening. I had the distinct feeling it was a cosmic play that I was allowed to view from the wings, so to speak. Since my reacquaintance with Pan, He informs me that it was He who guided me and attended the event in the operating room. The whole purpose of the incident was for me, and now you, to understand that we are not alone, and if unusual happenings are needed to achieve the cosmic goals in life, they still occur – perhaps all the time without our knowing.

Part of the life plan which you map out with the Old Ones and with spiritual consultants before you are born is how long you have been given to achieve your spiritual goals. In other words, you arrange for an approximate time to complete the learning process. Put another way, often our time to die is roughly predetermined before birth. In general, we are given a certain number of years, three, twenty, fifty, or seventy-five, to complete our assignment. When the task is done, or through inappropriate choices never will be accomplished in this lifetime, most check out and go forward to the next step in the learning cycle. Nobody dies prematurely. There are no accidents, and each person agrees to the life scenario. If your husband dies of a heart attack at the tender age of forty, rest assured that he followed his cosmic plan. And part of the plan is for you to experience the loss of your partner and learn to go on with life. Your children were consulted and understood prior to their birth that they would lose their father at an early age. This is part of their educational process as well. Perhaps, they need the experience to become more self-reliant. Whatever the specific circumstances, and regardless of how difficult it is and how much he will be missed, all those involved were consulted and agreements were reached at some level of their beings.

If you have a daughter killed in an accident at the age of twenty, understand that her time was up. For whatever reason, she only opted for twenty years to work out some problem or learn some life lesson. Since our egos are so closely identified with this particular physical existence, we fail to appreciate that any one physical incarnation is only a temporary platform for gaining wisdom through living as a body. Any human consciousness is vastly more complex and involved in a multidimensional existence than this one brief incarnation. You must accept your daughter's departure as an opportunity for you to learn as well. This is true whether you choose to accept the challenge or not, so you had best take advantage of the situation when it is presented to you. If you avoid the opportunity offered by her and refuse to go on with your life, grieving year after year, you deny the gift of her death.

Sometimes people ask how to determine if they have completed their Earthly job. The answer is quite simple. If you are still here, you have not completed what you came to do or learn.

It is quite common for the time of death to be open ended. I know one individual who was not fulfilling her potential and thus set herself up to die before the age of fifty-five. She was blocked in her spiritual growth, making no attempt to progress and holding to immature, reflexive patterns of social interaction with a tenacity that defied all reason. To continue was simply to draw her life out to no purpose. An event occurred when she was fifty-five that caused her to change her attitude. She began to work through her problem and accept the challenge of her life. She was given more time to complete the task of learning.

Ralph Warner told me of this experience which occurred in the fall of 1987. Two years before, he was called to see a man, dying of stomach cancer. His guide, Hector, instructed Ralph to lay hands on the man and heal him. Following the Reiki treatment, the fellow immediately improved. He started eating, gained weight, and remained healthy for many months. Two years after the healing his wife called, saying that his cancer had recurred and he was dying. He could not eat and was literally skin and bones, suffering terribly with his disease. She told Ralph that her husband would not allow himself to sleep for fear that he would die if he closed his eyes. Actually, she felt the only thing keeping him alive was his fear of death. She begged Ralph for his help.

Ralph found the man sitting propped up in bed. His eyes were bloodshot and red rimmed from lack of sleep. Ralph asked his guide, Hector, what he could do to help him. Hector told Ralph to hypnotize him, coax him out of his body, and talk him through the death experience. The man proved a good subject, and they continued to talk telepathically while the man described what was happening. At Ralph's urging, he went through the "tunnel" and passed into the light where he found himself on "the other side". There he saw several entities who appeared to be ordinary people. He became frightened, however, and fled back through the tunnel and reentered his body. Ralph did not know what to do next.

"Go with him," Hector commanded.

"What?" questioned Ralph. He was shocked at the suggestion. "That's called dying! Do you really expect me to go with him?"

166

"Yes, that is exactly what I want you to do. Get out of your body and take the man to the other side. Trust me."

Ralph said he had always done what Hector told him to do, so he got out of his body and led the man out of his. Together they walked hand in hand through the tunnel to the light. Ralph described the scene as "just like in the movies". There were flowers, green grass, trees, and a little brook. He said it was beautiful. Several people were there, and one elderly man walked toward them. The sick man was afraid, but Ralph convinced him it was safe to speak with the stranger. After a bit, he returned to Ralph, saying that he wanted to go back to his body. Hand in hand they returned through the tunnel and reentered their bodies.

Ralph went into the living room and spoke with his wife. He told her what had happened, relating that her husband had spoken with the older person. She asked what he looked like. As Ralph began to describe the individual, she stopped him. Producing a family photograph album, she began leafing through the pages. Suddenly, Ralph recognized one of the photos as the individual he had seen on the other side. It was a picture of the man's grandfather who had died before he was born.

Ralph returned to the bedroom and talked with the sick man. The fellow declared that he was no longer afraid to die now that he had met his grandfather. The next day the woman called to report that her husband died about two that morning with a smile on his face.

Remember the parallel pulse dimensions and your probable-selves? You are not the real one while the others are only theoretical. Each is a real one. It is only because of our intense focus in this existence that we are oblivious to the others. The totality of any one individual human consciousness is vastly greater than we are aware. Once you begin to grasp the enormity of it all, this particular moment of your total existence tends to fall into perspective. Life is vitally important, but the petty difficulties are truly insignificant when placed into cosmic perspective.

Most people want to know what happens when they die. The process of dying is not always pleasant, but at the height of the unpleasantness, the spirit simply steps out. Some deaths are quick while others take a long time. There are endless scenarios to explain why a slow death may be beneficial to the individual as well as to his family and friends. For one thing, a slow death allows loved ones an opportunity to become adjusted to the impending death. It also gives the dying person a chance to straighten out their business affairs, make a will, and other timely activities. In some situations, a slow death may be an act of love, allowing those left behind to face the loss with some feeling of relief. So, if one is experiencing a slow, protracted death, rest assured that the delay serves some purpose for the dying person – and perhaps others as well. Those who have learned their lessons concerning death or have nothing in particular to gain by experiencing a protracted death, usually have a quick way out.

Some senile individuals and those who are ill and experiencing periods of coma may spend considerable time out-of-body. Remember, we all go out-of-body during our dreams and have done it all our lives, so this is no great feat. For this reason, from their perspective, the exact time of death may be very hard to determine. With many, death is more like just failing to go back. Some enlightened souls simply step out of their bodies by their own volition and do not return.

While attending a conference in Italy, Karlfried Graf von Durkheim, a psychiatrist and author of a number of books on Zen Buddhism, told me of an event he witnessed while living in Japan during World War II. He was sent there as part of the cultural exchange program between Germany and Japan. One day, he was invited to a tea ceremony. Although he was told that it would be the Master's last tea ceremony, he did not fully realize the implication of that statement or what was to happen. The Master was a vigorous, spry gentleman in his upper eighties who appeared to be in the best of health. The guests sat quietly about while the Master made and served them tea, performing a flawless ceremony. After the tea ceremony was completed, he announced that he would give each of them a painting. A disciple, a man in his seventies, brought him ink, a bowl of water, brushes, and rice paper. Very deliberately the Master ground up the ink and mixed it with water. Then, taking his brush, he drew each of the guests a painting of a Zen monk sitting upon a lotus blossom. The marvel of each painting was that behind the monk he painted a halo, *a perfect circle.* To draw a perfect circle free hand is a tremendous feat of skill. Any slight tremble, hesitation, or doubt ruins the perfection of the circle. When the paintings were finished and each guest had been presented with one, the Master put aside the brush and ink and sat in the absolute stillness of meditation. Graf von Durkheim sat next to the Master. During deep meditation, the rate of breathing slows markedly. At first, it was not obvious what had happened, but after a span of about ten minutes, he noticed that the old man was no longer breathing slowly – he was not breathing at all. He looked more closely and saw that the pupils of his eyes were dilated and fixed. He was dead, sitting as he had before with a slight smile on his lips. What a way to go!

Normally, at death, the person's spirit simply leaves the body. At times, he may not even realize that his body has died, because from the perspective of the individual who dies, he does not even lose consciousness. The mind belongs to the spirit – the same mind that fuses with the brain when you incarnate. When death occurs, the mind simply detaches from the brain and from the body and continues functioning as before.

On occasion, there is a period of confusion. I hypnotized one man who was killed during the landing on Saipan in World War II. For a while, he ran about the beach attempting to get someone to listen to him. He tried to inform some officers that his Marine unit was receiving heavy fire. When they did not pay attention, he assumed it was because they were very busy. He did not realize he was dead until he passed through a palm tree as he ran along the beach. Even then, he was not totally convinced until he located his body lying face down in the surf and verified that it had been fatally wounded.

Everyone has heard or read accounts of near death experiences in which the soul passes through a tunnel and emerges into the light. This is essentially what all individuals perceive to happen although minor variations of the event are reported. Details of the experience tend to conform to what the individual expects. Those who are convinced they will go to hell often perceive ghastly figures and sounds of torment until they have a chance to adjust to the situation and learn differently. Devout Christians see entities they interpret as Jesus or angels – and indeed they may be. Elizabeth J. Eadie, in her marvelous book *Embraced by the Light*, described her visions in the metaphor of her fundamentalist Christian background. Muslims may be met by Muhammad. Buddhists may well be greeted by the Buddha himself. Usually, the individual is met by someone he knows or trusts just as it happened to the man with the cancer of the stomach who was met by his grandfather.

Eventually, each individual is taken before several of the Old Ones where a review of the entire incarnation is made. The review is not faultfinding, but nearly everyone is filled with regret for their petty, immature actions and behavior. There are no extenuating circumstances to hide behind. Everyone must accept accountability for their actions. During the debriefing, all the information and wisdom gained from the incarnation is integrated into all levels of the oversoul's involvement. Measured by linear time, this task may take several months or many years to complete.

Using hypnosis, I discovered that following the review each human spirit has several options available. This is not a unique finding of mine. Other investigators report essentially the same thing. The entity may elect to begin another incarnation as soon as his debriefing is over and suitable arrangements are made. There is the option of going somewhere to rest and do nothing. This is likely to happen if the person is not enthusiastic about learning. This choice has its limits, for the mandate is to learn and attain wisdom, and this is not accomplished, sleeping on a park bench and feeding the celestial pigeons. The third option is to attend school and obtain further education. There are cosmic classes available on all subjects critical to the development of the spirit and to aid in the success of various incarnational situations. If necessary, there are classes on very earthly subjects. Some of my patients told of studying psychology or medicine to insure the success of their next incarnation. One lady reported studying cosmic law. Every effort is made to assist the spirit in the learning process.

Unless the entity is finished with its incarnational cycle, it meets with the counselors to plan the next incarnation. This process is nicely outlined in the book by Whitton and Fisher, *Life Between Life*. Their book is based upon hundreds of hours of hypnotic interviews with patients. My experiences have been with numerous patients and friends with eight or ten hours of hypnosis per person at the most. Still, the information gathered is essentially the same.

The principle of multiple incarnations is unbelievably simple in concept yet infinitely complex and totally just. When viewed from the perspective of the Universe, there is no other system that would be as complete and afford the multidimensional platform for attaining wisdom.

Any and all contributions to the wisdom of the Universe are adequate. But, it is naive to think of one life's journey as being sufficient to explore the full potential of biologic participation. All experience has its own validity. Ultimately, nothing is wasted.

Salvation, according to Christian dogma, is thought to be a gift in return for loving God and accepting Jesus as one's savior. This is one view, but most religions hold similar beliefs as to the essential nature of their specific tenets and dogmas. *But a view may be correct without being the only correct view. From this incarnate perspective, all singular views are incomplete with rare*

171

exceptions. Additionally, a view may be personally correct, but not generally correct. The fact is that no religion has a valid claim as a sole source of knowledge or as the only vehicle for salvation. Many of the teachings of the various religions are identical to others. Mostly they deal with how man should relate to others and to the Universe. If mankind did not attempt to be something other than a man, quite likely there would not be the need for so many incarnations.

CHAPTER 7

Review of Concepts Presented

Throughout the book, I have introduced a number of ideas that may appear strange to the average reader. I know from experience that going over metaphysical material repeatedly is essential if one truly wishes to understand it and know how it applies to life. So, in an effort to make these ideas more easily understood, some of the concepts will be presented anew, using slightly different metaphors and methods of presentation.

Generally, what most of us think of as the Universe is limited to the view seen, gazing at the Milky Way on a clear night or those vistas provided by astronomers using telescopes and other means of seeing. Their photographs are awe-inspiring and leave us in wonder of its magnificence. However, these views are singular, narrow peeks at just one aspect of its being. In fact, only about seven percent of the consciousness composing the Universe is involved in its physical representation. It is said that if consciousness took up space, then the consciousness of a single cell would command an expanse the size of the Earth.

Through many hours of reading, conversations with my psychic friends and spending even more time in deep thought, I came to appreciate the Universe as a sentient being. This means that the Universe is an organized, huge something that is alive and has feelings. It is responsive to and interacts with psychic and emotional impressions. Therefore, it is entirely accurate and

173

appropriate to think of the Universe as a living, multidimensional entity composed of layer upon layer of intelligent consciousness, each relating with the others. Greg Satre confirmed this during a lengthy out-of-body experience that I mentioned in the first part of the book. Simply stated, the Universe is consciousness made physical by our intent.

At some time long past, mankind collectively chose to regard one aspect of this vast energy field as physical matter. So, it is through our intent that we perceive it as stars, planets, rocks, streams, plants, animals and various objects. Clearly, the world as we perceive it is an accurate view from our incarnate stance, but perhaps accurate from no other.

What we consider to be living beings are investments of spirit in plants and animals. But spirit, or consciousness, is the stuff of which everything is made. With this insight, it is obvious that consciousness is not confined to biologic forms of existence. Consciousness is consciousness whether it is in the form of an electron, a rock, a wisp of breeze, a rose, an ape, or a human. All is spirit, the consciousness of God – of the Universe. What separates the spirit of humans from that of minerals, plants, and animals is the way it is formed from the fundamental matrix of the Universe. Spirit can be compared to a deposit of clay from which any number of things can be created. Clay can be dug and shaped into bricks, pressed into decorative tiles, thrown on a potters wheel to make a vase, or sculpted into a figure. All four products represent different end results formed from the same clay. However, each evolved along different paths and has a unique purpose and function. Furthermore, a brick is not about to evolve into a tile or a vase into a sculpture.

Physiologically the body of man did evolve from the same biologic line as did apes, but human spirit did not. It is unique. When deciding whether a prehistoric creature was human or not, anthropologists focus upon the anatomical characteristics, equating form with humanness. But, it is not the size of the skull cavity, the shape of the dental arch and teeth, an opposing thumb, bipedal locomotion, or the facility to speak an oral language that separates mankind from primates. It is the presence of a human spirit that determines whether a creature is human or not. Human consciousness, as true of all consciousness, exists with or without a physical form. Furthermore, the shape and appearance of the physical body housing a human spirit is immaterial.

Despite what we are taught, humans do not have souls. We are souls. Nor can we lose our souls, for souls are what we are. We can, and do, lose our bodies through the process of injury or illness, but we cannot lose ourselves.

In considering these different ideas, keep in mind that our present view of the Universe is a correct view, but it is highly limited and not necessarily the only correct view. It is correct from this perspective but, perhaps, from no other viewpoint. In the same way, a truth is not necessarily the only truth. A truth can be personally correct but not generally correct. Again it depends upon one's perception.

As I have stated, the Universe is composed of interacting fields of intelligent consciousness. Regardless of statements to the contrary, some subatomic physicists seem to agree with this idea. Niels Bohr certainly did as well as Henry Stapp, Geoffery Chew, and others. They state that there are no such particles as quanta, electrons, protons, or atoms. They speak of psychological relationships that reach out to other relationships forming an endless network of consciousness. All else, all the things with which we daily surround ourselves and with which we interact, is a construction of our intent – costumes and camouflage of our dreams. We bring it into our physical reality by wanting it here. What makes this possible is that thoughts are tangible things. They exist as a form of energy resembling electromagnetic fields. (Greg Satre can actually see them.) Once formed, thoughts exist forever, remaining in a psychological matrix of intelligent consciousness.

We are intensely aware of our physical environment and daily activities. We surround ourselves at every moment with material objects, sights, people, animals, plants, and other things that comprise our tangible reality. While being aware of these things, we remain oblivious to the consciousness which forms them. In fact, most of us are oblivious of the other dimension altogether. We arise in the morning, eat breakfast, and go about our business. We think, plan, dream, and fantasize. We meet friends, go to work, go shopping, read a book, and all the other events, things, and activities with which we occupy ourselves on a daily basis. This everyday temporal association of mental and physical activities, and things make up our reality. It is called "Framework I."

But, this reality of everyday experiences and visible things does not represent the entire Universe – the real Universe. It consists of only those things and activities that we choose to have present. They are created from an infinitely vast psychological network of probabilities which is, in every sense, the real Universe. This network is called "Framework II." This dimension contains the potential of all things, possible events, beings, constructs, thoughts, probabilities, and probabilities of those probabilities.

To understand Framework II a bit better, consider this metaphor. As we create our environment and our lives, the probabilities in Framework II serve us in the same way that a dictionary serves an author as he sits down to write. Even before he begins, the dictionary holds within its pages his novel and every other novel, every article, every newspaper, every letter, and every thing that has been written or will be written. They are already there! The only thing the author has to do is to select the words he wants and place them in proper order. So, we see that the Pulitzer prize novel to be selected in the year 2015 is there printed in the dictionary, waiting to be brought into reality by the author's intent.

The everyday existence we call Framework I might be thought of as a dream reality. This tangible reality consists of various probabilities that we elect to actualize from the vastness of Framework II. Interestingly, the Australian aborigines believe that their earthly life and all that surrounds them is a shared dream and think of the dimension to which their spirit travels after death as the real world. The truth of the matter is that from a metaphysical point of view they are correct in this assertion.

As repeatedly stated, the Universe is made of intelligent consciousness. This is the basic substance of every atom whether it is an atom within a pebble, a plant, or an animal. You, too, are composed of the same intelligent consciousness. Some months ago I heard a learned professor of anthropology state on television that consciousness was a recent evolutionary development in the history of human evolution. The professor has much to learn despite his academic credentials. He needs to broaden his view of mankind and the Universe to include knowledge that lies beyond his narrow field of scientific study. He also denied that animals were conscious. I'm certain that as a boy he owned a pet. Did he truly believe that his dog or cat was not conscious? But, when he became educated, when he became a learned professor, he was blinded by his so-called scientific knowledge, allowing him to thrust aside his boyhood wisdom as childish nonsense.

Understand that mankind creates his environment down to the last detail and the Universe as he perceives it. I keep repeating this for it is crucial that this concept be understood. Some grasp of how it all works will answer many questions concerning the meaning of life, death, luck, coincidences and other confusing situations we face on a daily basis. The answers to these questions are unknown to most of us because of previously adopted beliefs that have been drilled into our minds over our lifetime. To aid understanding, multiple examples may help.

Since you chose to incarnate and experience the joys and the lessons that only can be learned living as a physical body, you need a world made of solid stuff. You require something tangible with which to create your body, food to eat and drink, material with which to build your home, and all other things necessary to experience your incarnation. Unless there is some way to create

177

matter from consciousness, there will be nothing with which to work. To this end eons ago, mankind, in total cooperation with the Primary Spiritual Being and all other entities – mineral, plant, and animal – chose a certain spectrum of consciousness with which to work. Then consciousness organized fields of electromagnetic energy about itself and, with focused intent and with unlimited cooperation from the Primary Spiritual Being, matter was formed. Had we decided upon a different construction, we might have built the Universe on other dimensions of energy, but our particular line of consciousness chose to construct it in the way with which we are familiar. So we build our houses with masonry, boards, and nails, all of which are nothing other than energy fields arranged as solid matter.

As you now know, the universe exists as an infinite number of psychological levels of consciousness. Although they are separate, they actually overlap and occasionally run together. No part of the Universe is truly separate from the rest any more than your liver is separate from your kidneys or your lungs. Each part has its unique function, but all join together for a common purpose and are part of a vaster organization called your body.

You are aware that thoughts are things that exist eternally as electromagnetic patterns of energy. So with this concept in mind, suppose you decide to invent some gadget. The moment you think of it, the idea exists in Framework II and will remain there as you modify it in thought. Then, through your focused intent, it takes form in this temporal reality as you construct it from plastic, metal, and so on. Once this is done, it becomes a reality for others as well. Any modifications of your invention remain in Framework II, waiting your decision should you decide to activate them.

Say you have a problem in your life that demands resolution. Every possible solution is already present in Framework II along with every outcome that may develop from the action you choose. No one forces you to select one course of action over another, but whatever course you take is already present in Framework II along with all possible consequences, and consequences of those consequences .... This gives validity to the old expression that "history is written in the stars."

As biologic entities, we are intensely focused in this reality and unaware of the activities that take place behind the scene. When you awaken in the morning, you create your day from the multitude of probable actions lying in wait. You could go to work or stay home. You might drive to the country, run your car into a utility pole, go to the grocery store, clean the closet, or any one of an infinite number of possible actions. When it is time for breakfast, you choose what you would like to eat from a multitude of probabilities in Framework II, but what you can eat is limited by what you have in the kitchen – the kitchen in Framework I.

Of the limitless potentials in Framework II, the ones not actualized are as real and as valid as the ones you select. Everything exists in thought whether they are ever brought into physical reality in this world or any other. Physical presence or observed actions and events are immaterial because thoughts are written in probabilities. All creative acts are conceptual, not physical.

Everything from a quantum to a human has a mind of one sort or another. Everything, and this includes rocks, rain drops, a weed in your garden, and the fly you swat, is conscious. They are also aware, communicate, have purpose, remember, dream, make plans, and are infinitely creative and precognitive within the constraints of their specific construct.

In humans and animals, the spirit fuses with the brain and nervous system, using this organ as a communicating device. One aspect of the mind concerns itself with the world outside the body. What is less understood is that there is an internal ego system as well. It is the part of the mind that is intimately associated with the workings of Framework II. It is through this subconscious connection with the infinite that we plan our lives through the mechanism of dreams. Every night we dream, acting

179

out various life scenarios along with others who are involved. Then we select the one that appears to be most advantageous for ourselves and the Universe and put it into action the next day. At times, we use our free will and do not follow our script. Usually this action serves our detriment.

In addition to this function, the internal ego maintains close communication with the consciousness of each cell in the body. Consequently, every person, though not aware of it, is intimately involved in the workings of his body. If we talk to our body, it will follow our suggestions. The cellular consciousness joyfully and continuously follows the commands of our mind.

Understanding the interrelationship between the Frameworks is so important that it should be restated in yet another way. At a conscious level, we decide what we want. Once the decision is made, the internal ego goes to work. In collaboration with our spirit guides and others who may be involved, arrangements are made to bring our desires to reality. Specific probabilities necessary to bring the plan to fruition are selected from Framework II, completing the process. To a large degree, the final result is dependent upon providing the greatest potential good for us, for others, and for the Universe.

In a way, our understanding of life is upside down. Our temporal reality can be thought of as a facade that we create from the vast array of possible events. What we consider to be luck or an accident is the inner working of Framework II being played out in Framework I.

Hard as this will be to accept, let me give a bit of information about the events of September 11, 2001. It will be discussed in the last chapter, too, but this may also be helpful in your understanding, Keep in mind that what I am about to explain took place at a subconscious level in Framework II. No one was remotely aware of the dynamics.

Prior to the event, the Universe felt that the United States should become actively involved, opposing the terrorist acts that were taking place about the world. As a nation, other than to condemn the actions, we refused to do much when our embassies were blown up, Marine barracks were destroyed, and the Cole was bombed. The thing needed to wake us up was a catastrophe on our soil.

All who died and were involved planned the entire event in Framework II. This included the hijackers as well as the passengers and the people who died in the buildings. Deep in their souls, the hijackers knew that their behavior was not in harmony with the purpose of the Universe. They made poor choices in life and locked themselves into a pattern of evil behavior and belief. It was time for them to begin anew. The others who died in the crashes chose to do so for the purpose of getting our nation involved. Those who were not killed did not agree to participate in this way and were spared by some "freak" of circumstances. When one understands the workings of Framework II, it all makes sense. Remember, there are no victims.

Everything that happens are events we create by our thoughts, dreams, and imaginations in Framework II and then attract to ourselves. This is true whether we are aware of our actions or not. This involves every event in our lives: the chance meeting of an old friend, finding a mate, taking a vacation, going to work, being fired, staying healthy, becoming ill, being shot by a crazed lunatic, or caught in an earthquake. At a subconscious level of knowing, we cooperate and help orchestrate the events in our lives – the successes, the failures, the joys, and the disappointments. With this knowledge, we are correct in saying that no one becomes ill or dies who does not wish to do so or is not in agreement with it happening. Nobody develops cancer, a heart attack, is killed in an accident or a drive-by shooting who at some level of their being did not plan it or agree to it. There are no victims, no accidents, no coincidences. It is only that we are unaware of planning them and of the intricate mechanisms by which they are produced.

Death always has purpose and meaning if we take the trouble to find it. Some people may choose to die at a particular time or in a particular way in order to make a statement. Elizabeth Eadie makes a point of this in her book *Embraced by the Light* as do Witton and Fisher in *Life Between Life*. For example, some who died in the race riots in Los Angeles and South Africa may have chosen to do so as a means of bringing attention to the social conditions prevalent in those areas. Perhaps they believed their deaths would make stronger statements than they could make in other ways. The same may be true of drug overdoses and violence. Political leaders may choose martyrdom through assassination, knowing they will have a greater influence on society through death than they could make by living.

But if we remain true to our beliefs, there is no such thing as a completely dead animal, plant, or person. Even after its spirit has departed, the atoms that compose its structure are still alive. They will remain alive and eventually be recycled into another being. And they will carry with them the knowledge of where they had been. The Universe is truly eternal. All this is a logical conclusion to the metaphysical beliefs that we have been discussing.

Since each of us creates our reality, an important question must be asked. If I create my reality and you create yours and everyone else creates their own, how do we manage to see and to experience the same things? Why is not the collective reality a jumble of confused events? The answer is that our realities are not identical. Each of us has a unique view of life although the differences are not great enough to notice, not usually anyway. The reason this can happen is that we are all in telepathic communication and reach and consensus of understanding of how things are to be.

This brings up another thing to consider. We are aware that Framework II contains all probabilities from which we select specific ones to form our temporal reality. Just as we all have our private realities, slight as the differences may be, we have individual Framework IIs as well. Once we incarnate, all probabilities are not available to everyone because we preselect the probabilities with which we intend to work before we incarnate.

For instance, the person who elects to incarnate into a life in an inner city slum and learn to face the challenges offered by that subculture must buy into the beliefs of that culture. To do otherwise would not be a true test and a learning situation. Therefore, the probabilities that he selects to work with are similar to those of his peers. To do as Nancy Reagan suggested and "just say, 'No' to drugs" doesn't make much sense despite being good advice. Perhaps he does not know anyone who has refused drugs. Surrounded by pushers and his friends urging him to participate, saying "No" is hardly an option. Refusing is not one of the probabilities in his Framework II. He can, if it occurs to him, select another probability and include it into his menu of probabilities, but it is not easy.

Another example may help. Suppose you decide to travel from your home to Miami, Florida. Prior to incarnating, you select the probability of going through life wearing dark tinted glasses. Now the map showing the routes from your home to Miami includes every road. The problem is that they are printed with varying shades of ink. Some routes are dark and easily seen while others are so faint that one has to study the map in bright light for them to be visible. With your dark glasses, there is no way for you to see the faintly printed roads.

Consequently, while you take the dark, easily seen route that leads to Miami via Mexico City, others wonder why you did not take the shorter, direct route that is printed with the pale ink. Since you preselected the option to wear tinted glasses, that route is unavailable to you because you cannot see it. You have the ability to dip into Framework II and select another probability which allows you to remove the glasses. But, you must first realize that other options are available and have the courage to make the change.

Everything from an electron, a rock, a plant, or an animal sees itself as the center of the Universe. From the viewpoint of your pet cat, a dandelion in your yard, a mosquito buzzing about your ear, or pebble in your driveway, you are part of its environment in the same way that you perceive it to be part of yours. Regardless of how it appears to be, we are truly inseparable. Each is a focus of individual consciousness within an infinitely vast continuum of consciousness.

What is more, each living thing, from a quantum to a man, actively seeks value-fulfillment, seeks meaning for its life. Each is conscious, aware, and intelligent in its own right, regardless of how insignificant we might consider it to be. Every creature, unique unto itself, has the same right to pursue and satisfy its life's purpose as do we. Each entity, be it a man, a worm, a wolf, or a tree has the same license to exist as every other. This statement is not to imply that a worm is as valuable as a human being or carried to the point where we hesitate to walk through the grass for fear of hurting the grass or stepping on an insect hidden there. Nor should it be taken to the extreme that we would choose to die rather than to kill some creature to insure our survival.

Clearly some organizations of consciousness are vaster than others. Within the system of the Universe, less vast organizations of consciousness are meant to willingly cooperate with and defer to the needs and desires of vaster entities. This is not to say that it must, for freedom of choice exists at every level of being throughout the Universe. This point is well made by Marlo Morgan in her book, *Mutant Message Down Under*. She gives a concise description of the way the group of aborigines with whom she was traveling went about their day. Each morning they had a group prayer and informed the Universe that a band of humans would proceed along a certain line of travel. In their prayer they asked permission to hunt and kill along the way in order to survive. Then they left it up to the plants and animals to decide among themselves which ones would sacrifice their lives for the benefit of the group. The marvelous thing was that they never failed to find sufficient food and water for their needs.

The concept of value-fulfillment has no specific definition. It is individually determined by each species and each individual. It entails a quality of life that goes beyond mere existence and survival. Value-fulfillment involves adding to one's life a depth of commitment, character, and purpose that goes beyond the minimum. Wild creatures will not live and reproduce in an environment that does not supply certain essentials which they feel are necessary to make life worth living for themselves and their offspring. This is the main reason for the disappearance of many species when the environment is altered. Zoo keepers had to learn what value-fulfillment means to each animal species and supply those things for them. The basics of food, water, and shelter are grossly inadequate for most creatures to survive.

Humans strive for value-fulfillment as well. Once various environmental requirements are met, value-fulfillment is attained through the satisfaction of living with honor and acquiring and maintaining certain principles and qualities in one's life. Value-fulfillment is measured by the depth and intensity of life's experiences – a vastness of being – rather than the broadness of involvement and possession of things. Eventually we must learn that things we desire or possess are far less important than most of us believe or suspect. Joining every club and activity that is available is not the answer either. We need to limit our activities so that the ones in which we do participate can be fully enjoyed.

When we fail to actively seek value-fulfillment, problems arise in our personal lives, our families, our communities, and nations. Social interactions become distorted and frequently individuals become mentally or physically ill. We cannot gratify the drive by attempting to model our lives after others. Each life serves a unique purpose that cannot be assumed by another. I must be myself. I cannot fulfill the destiny of another human being, nor can another fulfill mine.

185

Human entities, as true of all life forms, are created by the Universe from nondifferentiated consciousness. This is illustrated by the Biblical allegory of God creating Adam from nondescript dust. Since everything is part of the Primary Spiritual Being, it is accurate to state that all life is created from and is part of the spiritual consciousness that is the Universe.

Remember that all probabilities are present and viable at all times. Our existence in multiple foci and planes of reality is accomplished through our multidimensionality and the fact that time is relative. It is only from our biologic viewpoint that events occur in sequence. In this "eternal now" of relative time, using the words of Paul Tillich, "intensity of participation takes the place of a sequential time construct."

All of our lives, including this one of which we are aware, are but extensions of our oversoul. "Oversoul" is a term for the totality of our being, our "greater-self," that includes all of its extensions. The oversoul is eternal, but it is not static. It undergoes constant evolution and growth as each extension of its being gains wisdom in various arenas of instruction. The oversoul and the incarnational process might be thought of as an event in which discrete off-shoots of spirit extend outward from a central core and invest themselves into a number of unborn infants. Your present life represents one extension of this eternal core. Once incarnated each off-shoot, each soul, directs the growth of the body and develops its own attitudes, beliefs, and talents somewhat separate and removed from the oversoul. Upon the death of the body, the spiritual off-shoot is assimilated back into the totality of the greater self. However, this is not without exceptions.

A hateful, cruel personality is not received by its oversoul. This splinter must reincarnate any number of times, facing similar challenges until it learns to handle them without becoming vindictive or cruel. Then, and only then, will the off-shoot be reunited with its oversoul.

186

An incarnation is not an isolated event. While seemingly separate, it remains part of the oversoul and is in constant communication with it. In addition, it is in contact with extensions of itself in other time/space-separated dimensions of the Universe. Active interchange of experiences and knowledge takes place between the various extensions at all times. To a large degree, this happens in our dreams as we sleep.

To aid us in the learning experience, there are numerous spiritual entities available to help. These are often called "guardian angels" or "spirit guides." Not only are they accessible in our incarnate state, but available when we are disincarnate as well. If necessary, any number of vaster entities may assist in whatever manner is appropriate. Everyone has someone, but unless we ask, the guides may allow us to muddle through life without help or instruction.

Parents are chosen who are best suited to augment the specific learning situation. Every person has a voice in choosing their parents and, at the level of Framework II, the prospective parents are contacted and agree to have that particular entity be their child. If the infant is born a cripple, rest assured that the parents agreed to have a crippled child, and the child's spirit sought the situation.

One of my patients demonstrated to me a perfect example of this dynamic. She was a lovely, young girl who was a dwarf. Rita was a very bright, pretty child who was wise beyond her years. One day she asked, "Why me?" I explained that it was a challenge and that she chose this situation as a learning experience. I knew that in her next life, she intended to be a therapist working with retarded and crippled children. Her life as the dwarf afforded her complete understanding for the feelings and problems of patients she would meet in her next incarnation.

Every cell in the Universe is in communication with every other cell. The cells in your body are aware and have memory and purpose separate from, but in cooperation with, your spirit. This cellular consciousness takes instruction from your conscious and subconscious mind through the mechanism of your internal ego. Cells are not critical of these instructions. They tend to be much like small, obedient children in that, once given directions, they continue in that course until specifically directed otherwise.

In one context, the cellular-consciousness is a vast complex of memory, containing every isolated experience and perception. It holds these memories at the ready, waiting to infuse them into our experience of the moment. To give an example of how this works, if you suffer a difficult time or experience a traumatic event, your cells store the emotions and physical reactions associated with the ordeal. Years later, should something remind you of the past event, the cellular-consciousness floods your mind and body with the same emotions and physical reactions as before. The cells live in a timeless state and consider the trauma to be happening again. Not all cell memories are unpleasant. Gratifying and joyful experiences are retained by the same mechanism and affect us in their own way.

There is one more subject that needs to be reviewed by presenting it with a different metaphor of explanation. I speak of the theory of evolution. The simple fact is that, despite the story of evolution to which we have been indoctrinated since childhood, Darwin was wrong. Darwin drew inaccurate conclusions from his meticulous observations. His theory of natural selection plays a small part, but it does not explain evolution.

First of all, the myth of evolution begins with a fictitious, one celled creature that arose in the sea. Supposedly, this creature underwent endless mutations to produce more complex forms of life. The curious thing is that no one explains how the one-celled creature came to be or how it managed to become alive in the first place. Some years ago, a creative scientist came up with the idea that it floated to earth from outer space. This wild speculation is unlikely, but even it was true, this still does not answer the basic question of how it came to be alive.

Another problem with the accepted theory is the concept of relative time. Since time in the universe is in a timeless state, it is obvious that the entire creation occurred all at once. For this reason if no other, one form could not have given rise to another through the process of endless mutations over millions of years, at least not in the classic sense that we have been trained to view it.

To understand how the millions of varieties of creatures came to be, certain truths must be grasped. There are just three of them, but mankind has lots of problems accepting those truths. First, is the fact that the Universe is composed of consciousness and that consciousness creates matter and reality. Second, is the fact that thoughts are real things and exist forever in Framework II. Third, is that consciousness, in whatever form it takes, is creative and precognitive. These three truths answer all the questions about evolution providing you think of them acting in relative time and coupled with the fact that the creatures themselves play an essential role in their own creation.

In the beginning, the Primary Spiritual Being had a glorious explosion of creative exuberance. Strictly speaking it is not accurate to say "had" for the creation is taking place this second. The entire Universe, down to the last atom, is recreating itself at every moment. In any event, every element on the periodic table, every plant, animal, and human was created as a thought-form in one divine, inspired moment in the imagination of God. Existence is not dependent upon having a material form. There are marvelous creatures that have never been represented physically, yet they are as real and as fully created as you. More than a few species found that the environment on Earth did not meet their needs and chose not to return or to even appear in physical form at all. This is where Darwin's theory of natural selection comes to play. *The creation of anything is conceptual, not physical.*

As the thought-forms of the creatures sprang from the imagination of God, those thought-forms began having thoughts of their own, coming up with new variations of themselves. Each idea led inexorably to countless others. Therefore, in cooperation with the Pan aspect of God, plants and animals helped in their own construction. Using their precognitive abilities, they dreamed of their future and saw what form was required. They literally reprogrammed their genetic codes to produce the needed changes, just as the Galapagos finches did.

In a way, we see the same thing happening with our inventions. For example, think of the first airplane and then about all the flying machines that have been designed and constructed since. The various models were products of the designers' imaginations. But no one would be so naive as to think that in some way the Kitty Hawk evolved into a Boeing 747, gradually or otherwise. Those variations were created in the minds of the designers before the planes were constructed. In truth, there are plans for airplanes that will never be built, but they exist in Framework II, nonetheless, and are as fully created as the Stealth Bomber. The only difference is that when we talk about living creatures we don't think of them as being manufactured, but in a way they are. The aircraft were designed over a period of a hundred years by a number of engineers while the Primary Spiritual Being created everything in one incredible moment of inventiveness. So we see that the Biblical explanation of the creation is, in many ways, more accurate than the scientific one.

Hopefully, this repetition of ideas and concepts has been helpful. But we still need to investigate the benefit gained by understanding the metaphysical approach to life.

CHAPTER 8

Reincarnational Lessons

Any discussion of the nature of the Universe and multiple incarnations would be incomplete if it did not address the actual value to be gained from learning about our other investments of consciousness. One benefit from knowing these things rests in our ability to use the knowledge gained in other lives to guide us in this present one. Being aware of the reasons for our successes and failures can prevent us from stumbling about lost and confused, muddling through life. Even though we may not know specific details of our other incarnations, certain belief that multiple lives do occur can serve much the same function. This information places us in a unique situation by giving a broader, more discriminating view of our existence, the Earth on which we live, and the Universe of which we are a part.

In the last few years, it appears that nearly everyone is curious about "past" lives. The number of people totally opposed to belief in reincarnation is less now than before. More and more books on the subject appear in print. Much of this renewed interest is due to the courage of Shirley MacLaine and her willingness to write about her personal quest for wisdom in the book, *Out On a Limb*. She followed this with a movie based upon the book and wrote several more on metaphysical and occult subjects. Bless her.

While television programs about metaphysical subjects and references to reincarnation are commonplace, most of the material presented is quite superficial. Some is presented for no other purpose than to ridicule and refute the validity of these subjects. Despite the skeptical tone of many commentators, the programs are aired and people talk and theorize about them.

For years, I maintained that if we were supposed to know about our other incarnations, we would have been designed to do so from the start. Therefore, the increased interest was little more than curiosity – the newest craze like asking a stranger about their astrological birth sign. Some years ago, Greg led me to realize that originally we were meant to recall our other lives, but we gradually repressed that ability.

We have walked the path of spiritual non-awareness to the point that its flaws are patently evident. Remember the Lumanians who endeavored to evolve spiritually in a nonviolent direction? They ultimately found that total nonviolence was incompatible with continued existence as a biologic creature on Earth. Even a tree will prevent other trees from competing with it for water and nutrients. It does so with its shade. Other trees, except those that have adapted to a low-light environment, have difficulty growing in the shade of larger, mature trees. Desert shrubs, such as mesquite, extrude a chemical from their roots to prevent other plants from germinating or surviving within their territory. Pinon pine trees prevent other pines from competing for moisture and nutrients by creating an energy field about them that prevents seeds from germinating. Some form of confrontation is inevitable for any creature to survive. As you recall, most of the Lumanians simply left Earth, and those who were not as advanced in the direction of nonviolence stayed behind and forced themselves to leave their underground cities. They interbred with other humans in the hope that their offspring would have stronger instincts to fend for themselves.

However, we must not use this knowledge to justify a hostile, confrontational stance. Life is not about winning or losing – about being right or wrong. It is about learning to get along and allowing others the opportunity to seek their destinies.

Differing opinions can be held without assuming that if one is true the other must be false. Every disagreement need not be resolved with one person victorious and the other ground down into the dust of defeat. Both sides may hold an element of truth, and the opposing views may simply represent a paradox designed to lead us to a greater truth. Hundreds of years ago, the Afghan philosopher, Jelaluddin Rumi, made this statement about confrontations. "Out beyond right doing and wrong doing, there is a field. I will meet you there." Of course, the field to which he referred is the field of free and open debate where no one is expected to win or lose and where blame is not placed. Rarely does blame need to be assigned nor do opinions need be defended.

At some level of spiritual comprehension, we human beings must come to grips with the fact that we need to alter our attitude and our behavior. One thing that will enable us to change will be the acceptance of the truth that we live more than one life. *Mankind must evolve in a different spiritual direction – one that includes memories or, at least, the concept of other incarnations. We must learn from those experiences and heed their lessons. This is critical!* Due to our ignorance of other lives, we fail to understand and empathize with those of different beliefs, races, religions, cultures, and sex. If we knew of our other incarnations, it would be more difficult to hate and abuse others. Once accepted, the reality of multiple incarnations will lead to our learning compassion and tolerance.

In the meanwhile, we should continue to address the problems and difficulties we see about us. *But, while acknowledging that these problems exist, we must not dwell upon them or grant them undo attention. This is extremely important. If we are to change ourselves and society, we must quit emphasizing those things that we wish to overcome by constantly thinking and talking about them.* One does not attain peace through the act of hating war. We attain peace by loving peace. We cannot eliminate violence by hating violence and

193

waging battle against the perpetrators of violence but by rewarding gentleness and kindness. We influence others to be compassionate by honoring those who show concern, not by despising individuals who show indifference. These statements are supported by principles learned in previous chapters that thoughts truly are things, as real as rocks and trees, and exist unto eternity as electromagnetic fields of energy in Framework II. *When we dwell upon negative things, similar thoughts cluster about, adding strength and permanence to the very behavior we wish to eliminate. Clearly, we must not emphasize the negative aspects of life and the behaviors we wish to abolish but concentrate, instead, upon those qualities we wish to achieve as individuals and as a society.* After all, it is common knowledge that we cannot teach a dog to come to us when we call by whipping him each time he fails to obey the command. We gain his active cooperation and his love by rewarding him when he does obey.

Often, those who view the "other side" through near death experiences, meditation, or psychic intuition, return to this temporal reality saddened by what they see about them – a milieu of crime, corruption, hate, violence, greed, despair, and sorrow. Some are depressed at the need to remain here and wish to return to that dimension of love and peace. But, the challenge of being incarnate is to make this dimension one of love and concern as well. We are summoned to structure Earth into the "Eden" we view on the other side. This is best accomplished by concentrating upon those qualities of life that we wish to attain. Unfortunately, we have conditioned ourselves to do just the opposite.

No doubt early man was not unlike animals in one respect. He remembered other incarnations and consciously built upon those experiences. Somewhere along the way, he came to view the recalled memories as mere fantasy and therefore invalid. Over time, he suppressed the memories of other lives. As a consequence, mankind evolved for hundreds, perhaps thousands, of years isolated from its spiritual center, unaware of other lives let alone the details of those lives. He deluded himself into a false state of superficial contentment isolated from his inner being – and with disastrous results.

You recall the discussion which likened the human spirit to a torus, acquiring information from Framework II by means of its internal ego connections, processing it, and then returning it to society through the external ego and its outer involvement. *When we allow ourselves to be cut off from our inner-self by practiced avoidance of introspective activities, we stifle our ability to perform our primary objective as human beings. We often block our opportunity to attain wisdom and value-fulfillment.*

Acquiring practical knowledge of the world is not in itself a bad thing. Indeed, it is a useful and a necessary function in this temporal existence and, in one sense, why we are here. The mistake came when we turned completely aside from developing our intuitive knowledge as well. In general, we ceased giving any inward glance toward understanding our psyche and how we should structure our lives.

Again, we can use the Lumanians as an example to illustrate the need for balance in life and in our culture. They attempted to evolve into a totally nonviolent race while failing to realize that the ideal goal is to maintain a dynamic balance. They reached a point where they could no longer tolerate confrontation of any kind. Carried to extreme, nonviolence became undesirable. It would have been just as futile to evolve into a race that was totally violent. This experiment would not have reached its goal either, for they would have fought and killed until none were left to continue the race. Again, the answer is a dynamic balance. We know that each value has an opposite value. Good and evil, love and hate, concern and indifference are not in opposition to each other. Clearly, they define one another, each enabling its counterpart to exist.

I give us credit for one thing. We are very creative when inventing reasons to hate and ways to get even. Since we work at this so diligently, one might conclude that we made this sort of behavior a cultural goal. This must cease.

We find ourselves at a turning point in our evolutionary path. Fortunately, it appears we are beginning to realize the importance of knowing about our other lives and the various races and cultures we experienced as those individuals. This knowledge and the absolute recognition and acceptance of the fact that we are spirits enjoying a brief sojourn as a physical body will go a long way toward reshaping our world and our culture. Awareness of these things may be the salvation of this line of human consciousness.

In ages past, long periods occurred when the external ego was not so empowered towards separation from the rest of the mind – or may not have even existed. We must set about, reeducating our external ego and modifying its temporal demands in order to regain our spiritual balance. Fortunately, we have not permanently locked ourselves away from contact with our inner being, and awareness may be regained with desire and focused intent.

All organizations of consciousness are basically experimental in the true sense of the word. The Lumanians and the Atlanteans were very knowing in ways other than biological interaction. Even today, some primitive societies such as the Australian aborigines or isolated Indian tribes in the Amazon basin are very knowing and enlightened in their own fields of expertise.

Through our desire to remain unaware of other incarnations, we have done much the same thing to ourselves that we do to animals when we domesticate them. The process of domestication involves raising wild animals in captivity for generations until their spiritual memories dull to the point where they have all but forgotten their wild ways. Once their old behavior patterns are suppressed through disuse and new ones established, we say that the animals are domesticated. Initially, domestication involves mutual cooperation between the creatures and mankind – and still does. Animals that reject domestication do so by refusing to cooperate and reproduce. If kept in captivity, they simply die or remain wild. A crocodile cannot be domesticated simply because it does not want or need human companionship. It views us as just another potential meal. But even in domesticated creatures, memory of the wild behavior is never totally lost. The potential is always there, and any domesticated animal will revert to the wild if given time and the proper circumstances.

Applying this analogy to man's situation, it is clear that for countless generations we actively suppressed knowledge of, and contact with, our spiritual selves. Over time, the connections within the brain that enabled us to *consciously* remember other incarnations and their associated lessons withered from disuse. Neurologically, the nerve connections that carried this information became disengaged. As we avoided contact with our spiritual self, we lost some degree of control over the external ego. In one sense, it began to take on a life of its own. The external ego aspect of the mind continued to develop and expand as it interfaced with the temporal reality. Unfortunately, this was done without the moderating influence of the eternal ego. This is the state in which many of us find ourselves as the external ego function runs amok, doing what it pleases regardless of the effect on others. But this forgetting is true only at conscious, waking levels. The spiritual self is fully aware of our other commitments of being at all times.

It is through the mechanism of the internal ego that we tap into the vast field of unselected probabilities – that information base called Framework II. The internal ego function maintains contact with our other investments in consciousness. It is only our ability to consciously recall these events that faded. For many generations, we told ourselves that believing in multiple incarnations was silly and unscientific. Today, many people are convinced that even discussing the subject is sinful. Over time, the recall mechanisms became less and less effective. What you do not use, you tend to lose. Fortunately, some are still about who are not so spiritually "domesticated".

Each of us can be consciously aware our spiritual center if we have the desire and the resolve to do so. The intuitive powers are only latent, not gone, and the ability to recall other incarnations can be activated with desire and practice. Unconditional, focused intent is required for change to be made, enabling us to return to our natural state and "undomesticate" ourselves. The dormant neurological connections will become more easily activated as each succeeding generation imprints on the genetic code and the cellular consciousness its intent to know these things. Indeed, with sincere intent, some individuals can reactivate this function within a span of a few months or years just as the Galapagos finches altered their bill structure. In the process, we must refrain from punishing, ignoring, or ridiculing our children when they relate their intuitive insights. Indeed, these activities should be accepted in a matter-of-fact manner.

One of the people with whom I did some past life recall – the man who remembered being the little plant in the forest – told of an experience with his five year old daughter. One evening, she approached him very seriously, but with suppressed excitement. He was reading the newspaper and, although he was not disinterested, he was not giving her his full attention.

"Daddy," she said, "I know something that nobody else in the whole world knows!"

"Yes?"

"First, you're born and you're a little baby. Then you grow up and you grow old. Then you die. Then you're born again, and you're a little baby all over."

"That's nice dear," he responded.

Apparently, he did not seem to be adequately impressed for she stamped her foot and exclaimed, "Daddy, you don't understand!"

She proceeded to get her doll and act out the birth, death, and reincarnation scenario for him. This time, he responded by telling her how much he appreciated her letting him in on the secret. Later, when he related this incident to me, I asked if she could possibly have heard him discussing his hypnotic revelations with his wife. He replied that was not a possibility, for he had barely mentioned them to her, and their daughter had not been around. The latter response to his daughter was the appropriate one and one that we all should give. He listened, he took her seriously, and he let her know that he did.

Maya Angelou once said that the most important single attribute a person needed was courage. She went on to explain that, without courage, no one could be the sort of person they wanted to be – at least not consistently. She said that a person might want to speak out against racial prejudice, for example, but without courage, the moment their position was threatened they were very apt to recant or modify their objection. Maya Angelou is right in her assertion, but there is something even more basic and that is a sense of self-worth. Courage is possessed only by individuals who are secure in the truth of their own value. Self-validation stems from the knowledge that one is totally acceptable, a unique human being and one with the Universe.

The easiest and most effective way for an individual to gain certainty of his self-worth is through the love and nurture of the parents. Supportive, loving parents are the greatest gift one can have. Because my parents steadfastly reinforced their belief in me, I believed in myself. From this base of confidence, I had the courage to achieve the things in life I felt destined to do. Without the courage that stemmed from a deep conviction in my personal value, I could not have been the unconventional person I am and learned the things I have.

In the meantime, it is critical for all persons to accept the undeniable fact that they have been members of both sexes and, more than likely, members of different races and cultures. We are one, and we have been all. To quote Pogo, "We have met the enemy, and they are us."

If my great grandfather was killed by a Sioux Indian in the

course of forcing them from the Black Hills in the 1800s, this does not give me reason to hate my neighbor simply because he happens to be an Indian. More than likely, my neighbor has done nothing to cause me to dislike him. He may even be a friendly fellow who has gone out of his way to be neighborly. What happened to my great grandfather has nothing to do with me – maybe. Considering the way souls often change races from incarnation to incarnation, I might have been the Sioux warrior who killed my great grandfather. It is possible that my Indian neighbor was my ancestor in that particular life, and we are getting another opportunity to relate to each other in friendship rather than in hate. And, if we do not solve our differences, it is possible that my spirit and that of my neighbor may work out our karmic relationship as husband and wife at some other time. Biologic roots have little meaning except to add a flavor of cultural history to life and sometimes the color of the hair, eyes, or skin to a particular individual. How could I, a white man in my present incarnation, hate black people? This is true for two reasons. First, my parents were not prejudiced toward people of other races, and second because I remember that I was a Haitian in the life before this one. I recall it clearly.

I am amazed at the attitudes of people who believe that simply because their biologic ancestors were treated badly in the course of history that society owes them some special treatment. Lots of groups – racial, ethnic, and religious – have members who hold this belief. Feuds and vendettas go on for generations over some incident that happened so long ago that the details are all but forgotten. The list is endless. To illustrate the silliness of these attitudes, I offer the following actual case history.

When I was practicing medicine in Bellaire, Ohio, one of my patients was a black man who had been a coal miner. He was disabled because of a work-related back injury. We decided to determine if hypnosis might afford him relief from his constant pain. I had him come to my home where he could stretch out on the couch and not be disturbed. Jim was not a big man, about five foot nine and weighing 145 pounds, yet when he worked in the mine, he considered himself equal to any task that required heavy lifting. Under hypnosis, I did some past life investigation with him, thinking there may have been another life in which he injured his back. Memories of injuries or illness in one life often influence recovery of similar events in another. In his immediate past life, he worked on a railroad, laying track. He was a gigantic black man capable of breaking railroad ties by snapping them over his knee. Jim's present injury resulted from carrying the psychic memory of having a monstrous body that could lift anything. Then I suggested he go to the incarnation before that one.

"Where are you living?"

"In Nashville," he replied. Without hesitation, Jim gave me a street address.

"How old are you?"

"I'm nineteen."

"Are you male or female?"

"I'm a guy."

"Are you black or white?"

Jim exploded with rage and screamed, "I'm no damned Nigger! My buddies and me go around looking for Niggers to beat up just for the fun of it. Hell no! I'm no God damned Nigger. I'm white!"

"Jim," I cautioned. "Listen to yourself. Listen to what you're saying."

"I said I was no damned Nigger!" he screamed. "Oh...Oh, my God ... my God, Dr. Bonnett, I never understood before."

Gradually, he calmed down as the emotion and hate drained away from him.

"What finally happened to you?" I asked.

"I was killed when a huge packing case fell out of a window and landed on me. I have an idea that someone pushed it out of the window on purpose. I was twenty."

Out of hypnosis Jim was quiet, saying nothing for a long

time. He was obviously thinking about the memories and prejudices he had unearthed. After a bit of reflection he said, "Thanks, Dr. Bonnett, I never understood prejudice before." He went on to explain that he did not understand why someone would dislike him when they had never met. He could not imagine their reason or motive. He went on to say that recalling the life in Nashville helped him understand. There were no reasons! When he had been the white youth, the prejudicial beliefs were imprinted into him by his mother and father at birth and continued to be infused into his belief system by childhood associates and others by their repeated remarks and their attitudes. The hatred seemed to be innate, and he had never thought to question it.

Jim was right. When we enter an incarnation, we need help and direction concerning our stance in society. Just as a gosling imprints on the first thing it sees move and believes it to be its mother, human infants do the same except that the imprinting goes much further. Humans imprint on the mother's attitude toward life, the manner in which she views the world and the culture, whether she is trusting or suspicious of others, and many other things. It is evident that we do not need to speak about our hates and our prejudices to our children in order to influence them. They are aware of our feelings and beliefs from the day of their birth, indeed, from the moment they select their parents.

Each life, though it is but a moment in the continuum of eternity must, in one sense, stand alone. To be a true framework in which to learn, it often needs to be experienced from the perspective of that specific life and, to a degree, in isolation from other incarnations. It is, nonetheless, critical for one to make other life connections and correlate them with the present. This is done on a nightly basis in dreams and through subconscious memories. At least until now, this is the way it has been, but many are starting to realize that these subliminal reminders are not enough. We are so blind to the recalled information of former lives that it has little effect on us. The bit that does creep through

202

to conscious levels is ignored or not trusted. So we continue on with our hatred, our misunderstandings, our prejudices, and our ignorant ways. If we were aware of other incarnations, it would be difficult to be mindlessly prejudiced toward others, for knowledge gained in one incarnation could easily carry over into another.

Death completes all incarnational journeys. Either the purpose of the incarnation was fulfilled, or it was not going to be as a result of exercising our free will and making unwise choices. One problem in our culture today is that there is scant opportunity or time to jump probabilities. As the culture becomes more complex, it is difficult to break free of customs and the solidified expectations of others. Additionally, the task is more difficult due to a lack of waking, conscious awareness in our lives. For these reasons, departing this life becomes a practical way of solving the dilemma. It allows one an opportunity to achieve a more fulfilling result in the next. Sometimes death of an individual is attained by joining a group in death. Therefore, through the act if dying, a group or an individual may be jumping probabilities and allowing themselves to participate in a different, more fulfilling incarnational direction. Previously I gave one example of the need to jump probabilities with the story of my friend who could not ignore the demands and expectations of others and attend to her own needs. There are many variations.

I am told that the purpose of mass deaths such as natural disasters, plane crashes, and the like sometimes serve as a type of balancing or evening-up process. Apparently, there are times when it is more important to have these souls free of their Earthly entanglements and available for some cosmic purpose than for the individuals to complete their present lives. Pan informs me that people who die in mass disasters often have some close karmic connection and are fulfilling a purpose of which only they and the gods are aware. Others, not involved with the karmic group, simply take advantage of the opportunity to die for their own reasons, booking passage on a plane destined to crash or rushing to the site of an impending disaster to be caught in it.

Some mass events such as the terrorist attack of September 11, 2001 that involved several airplanes and resulted in the death of thousands were arranged for the specific purpose of gaining the attention of our country. Other terrorist events had failed to adequately get our collective attention so those who died planned the event in Framework II. They realized that it was critical to the world that we join others in fighting terrorism. Dying in that manner, to insure that we would become involved, was more important than finishing their individual incarnations.

Another reason for mass deaths is that technology and medical advances are making it increasingly difficult for people to die of what used to be considered natural causes. Pneumonia, infantile diarrhea, measles, small pox, and other infectious diseases no longer kill people as frequently as they did before antibiotics and vaccines were developed. On the down side, advances in medical technology make dying of common illnesses much more difficult. What used to be a quick, relatively painless death a generation or two ago is often a drawn out, distressing, miserable, and a costly ordeal. Automobiles are safer and many survive crashes that in other times were fatal. Examples are almost endless.

Rest assured, people will die of something when they wish to go regardless of what we do or the precautions taken. If medical science suddenly discovers a cure for cancer, AIDS, and heart disease, the total number of deaths each year from all causes will be unchanged. For these reasons, people who desire to check out often find it easier to use disasters and plane crashes to fulfill their purpose.

In the event of a mass catastrophe, should there be some compelling reason why a certain person needs to continue with this particular life, that individual will be spared. That will be the person who has a flat tire on the way to the airport and misses the plane, or plans are suddenly changed, the flight is overbooked, or as we observed, the one man on top of the World Trade Center who rode the building down as it collapsed and was rescued. In the bombing of the federal building in Oklahoma City, certain people were not killed because of some circumstance that delayed their arrival to work, or something led them to make an uncustomary trip to another portion of the building. We all hear stories of this nature. When this occurs, understand that those individuals have important personal reasons to complete this life.

On occasion, political or religious leaders may elect to be assassinated in order to make stronger statements than they could achieve by living. By becoming martyrs, their followers continue with renewed vigor to accomplish their goals. At other times, a child may choose to be killed in a drive-by shooting. Through their death they may feel they can make a bold statement concerning the status of the society. Indeed, the opportunity to die in this fashion may be the primary reason for a particular incarnation. Keep in mind that all these things are arranged in that network of probable interactions we have called Framework II, and everyone involved is included in the planning.

I am concerned about the huge number of individuals on Earth who are experiencing their first one or two incarnations. These people are not unlike three year old children. No matter how charming and intelligent they may be, they are no more capable of making wise decisions about life than a three year old is capable of knowing what is best for him. A little child needs parents to tell him to eat his vegetables, drink his milk, and when to go to bed. The frightening thing is that these "three year olds" may direct giant corporations, hold high public offices, or are individuals of great influence. These new souls have no sense of good judgment and refuse to listen. At this time in history, there are so many of them, and so few old souls around, that the potential is there to upset the balance of this entire evolutionary endeavor.

On the other hand, some incarnational immaturity is due not to "new" soul function so much as newness to this format and the headiness of a highly empowered, external ego with which they

205

have little experience. The materialistic attitude prevalent at this present time becomes very intoxicating to the uninstructed personality in this society – a society which actually encourages immaturity in many of its structures. In fact, greed based societies thrive on immaturity. Nevertheless, this present culture with its numerous problems offers a great opportunity to learn and gain wisdom in a quick, intense wave of challenges.

Many television programs have a powerful negative effect on our society despite some opinions to the contrary. The industry is quick to claim credit for culturally uplifting programs of sporting events, concerts, dramas, and so on. Yet, it denies that the less wholesome ones are detrimental. Since its invention, it has undergone some changes in programming that are very destructive to society. At least, this is my opinion. In the past, television aired some marvelous programs such as Father Knows Best, The Donna Reed Show, Leave It to Beaver, and others. Today they are often ridiculed, put down in a backhanded manner, or damned with light praise by saying that they were alright in their way but did not represent actual life situations – they were not relevant to our times. *What they did show were people resolving problems with reason and respect for one another and without resorting to violence.* Programs such as these have all but disappeared.

Reasonableness and respect for others are attributes that we must demonstrate to our children if we are going to solve the epidemic of violence. We must demonstrate to our children how much we love them and how to resolve differences without violence. Waiting until a child has injured or killed another is delaying the educational process far too long. *It must start the very first time one toddler pushes or hits another toddler or calls the other a name.* Despite the euphemism that psychologists and psychiatrist like to use, that the children are merely "acting out their frustrations", such behavior is nothing less than violence, and it must not ever be dismissed as insignificant or harmless. Childhood is the age at which social behavior is learned, and we must help them learn to handle their frustrations and differences in a civilized manner.

As mature human beings, we need to realize that part of attaining wisdom is the knowledge and application of reasonable discipline. Discipline at the metaphysical level is for the purpose of learning to make compassionate, enlightened, constructive choices. This ability is the core of wisdom in action. This is the intended goal of human endeavor, and if we are aware, this knowledge can be carried from one incarnation to another.

Years ago, I hypnotized a man who recalled a life as a member of the French Foreign Legion. He had no family, so upon retirement, he remained in an Arabian village near the fort where he eventually died a lonely old man. One day he confided in me, saying that he had been offered another job with a salary over twice what he was making. It was a very attractive offer. The only problem was that the new job would require him being away from home for extended periods of time. A week or so later, I asked if he intended to accept the new position. He said that the night before, he had been lying in bed, pondering his decision. For some reason, he thought of his life as the Legionnaire, and he vividly recalled how lonely he had been. Accepting the new position meant that he would miss taking part in family activities and seeing his two sons grow up. He said that one life of loneliness was enough, so he turned it down.

Like the oak tree that was content to be an oak rather than a pine, we should not go about unhappy with our status in life, feeling we are victims. We must not forget that we choose and create life's situations, good or bad. Problems should be met with the excitement of adventure, knowing that we are the authors of those problems. Since we create our lives, we have the power to reshape them as we choose. Life is to be enjoyed while we learn our lessons and attain wisdom. The Earth is our field of play, our gymnasium in which to romp and frolic while we learn to get along, learn and grow wise.

Usually, when life becomes difficult it is caused by our failure to make wise choices. Even illness, with rare exceptions, is the result of failing to fulfill our greatest constructive potential. When we go against the grain of life, we find progress difficult. When mankind listens to his conscience and acts with maturity of spirit, life flows as easily as water in a stream even if there are occasional boulders in its path.

If mankind were more conscious of his incarnational past and future, we would be aware of the karmic lessons, waiting to be learned. Perhaps we would recall being residents of some third world country, seeing ourselves exploited and remembering how we felt. We would know how it feels to be despised for the color of our skin, our style of clothing, our accent, or our religious belief. We would learn from the Lumanians and realize that certain stances are incompatible with life. We would reflect upon other world cultures that were destroyed on other occasions by many of the same practices that we indulge in today. We would remember why those dimensions had to be abandoned and human life on Earth was required to start over from scratch.

Awareness of the truth of multiple incarnations would make it possible to see ourselves from the perspective of the Universe. Knowledge of other incarnations would prevent us from leading desperate existences. The sad truth is that most of us do lead lives of desperation simply because we fail to listen to our inner voice and remain ignorant of the truth of multiple incarnations. Our desperation and discontent is self-made.

It is unnecessary for huge numbers of people to know of other lives and their karmic connections to achieve some degree of transformation. The only requirement is for the majority of people to understand the truth and the meaning of the incarnational cycle we experience, and act accordingly. To use an analogy, we do not have to know what engineering principles were utilized in the construction of a bridge in order to drive over it. On the other hand, simply because we are ignorant of them, we do not deny that certain engineering principles were used in its making. Mankind must become aware of, and incorporate into his belief system, the incarnational principles of the Universe. Beyond that, he must start acting upon that truth as to be compatible with the wisdom and knowledge contained in such a belief.

We are responsible for ourselves. Knowing of our other incarnations should impart a strong sense of humility and empathy for others. However, personal experience is not the only way to gain wisdom. At times, it is not even the best way. It is not necessary to jump off the Empire State Building to learn that there are better ways to get down to street level. There are other methods to learn besides personal experience. One of the best ways to wisdom is through intelligent, thoughtful observation. It can be achieved by observation of others, or intelligent, mindful scrutiny of our own actions. Unfortunately, experiencing various life events does not insure that we are observing ourselves or aware of the significance of our acts. Too often, our lives are mindless and serve no function in the quest for wisdom. We all know adults who, except for being able to button their coats and tie their shoestrings, are no more mature in terms of civilized interaction with others than they were when they were three. It is quite obvious that multiple incarnations are necessary as each human consciousness proceeds onward in its adventure of learning.

By presenting these ideas about the cosmos and human nature, I have not detracted from the wonder and majesty of your Universe. I hope I have opened your eyes to new concepts. I have offered a picture of The Primary Spiritual Being that is far grander in scope and dimension than many of you have dared to imagine. We all need to open our minds to the wonder and the multidimensional nature of God and acknowledge that we are a part of that God. We must cast aside any narrow, rigid belief system that is so closed and sealed that new ideas cannot find a crack in which to enter. We need to abandon our fear to think and have the courage to be ourselves.

O.T. Bonnett is a retired physician, a published author, and a sculptor. He was born in 1925 in Salina, Kansas and grew up in Kansas, Wyoming and Illinois. He graduated from University of Illinois College of Medicine in 1948. After his internship and two years of general surgery residency, he was activated into the Navy during the Korean war, serving for two years. The first eighteen months he was attached to the Second Marine Division at Camp LeJeune, North Carolina, and the last six months he was in charge of a thirty bed surgical ward at the U.S. Naval hospital there.

Following military service, he entered general practice in Champaign-Urbana, Illinois. He practiced eighteen years as a solo practitioner, delivering babies, performing major surgery, and all the things associated with being a general practitioner. In the fall of 1970, he joined The Bellaire Medical Group, an HMO based in the coal fields of West Virginia and Ohio where he served as Chief of the Department of Adult Medicine. In 1987 he left active practice and assumed a position as Medical Director of Miners Colfax Hospital in Raton, New Mexico. He retired after five years and began writing books.

In the fall of 1987 while exhibiting his sculpture at an art show in Denver, he met Greg Satre who had a pottery booth next to him. He says their meeting was one of the most significant events of his life, ranking with his birth, graduating from medical school, and meeting his spirit guide, Pan.

Throughout his entire life, he has been interested in philosophy and metaphysics. As a boy, he read Emerson and Lao Tse. Many metaphysical principles were incorporated into his practice. Some fifty years ago, through the use of hypnosis, he learned that we all experience multiple incarnations. This knowledge, coupled with metaphysical principles, was helpful in the recovery of many patient's illnesses and injuries.

Dr. Bonnett published two scientific articles: *Effects of Positive Suggestion on Surgical Patients* and *The Treatment and Prevention of Acute Dysionic Myocardial Necrosis*. In addition, he is the author of two published books: *Confessions of a Healer* and *Why Healing Happens*.

The first forty-five years of his life he was deeply involved with the Presbyterian church. He attended Sunday school and church regularly and was an elder for many years. Various experiences led him to adopt a different stance in life.

He and his wife, Hazel, live in Raton, New Mexico with their two cats, Barney and Zoro. Their home is as ancient 125 year old dwelling which they remodeled and redecorated, doing much of the work themselves. He enjoys the solitude and the wide expanse of the eastern slope of the Rocky Mountains where bear and deer are frequent visitors to his yard, not to mention the many species of birds that come to his feeders.

O.T. Bonnett
PO Box 1272
Raton, NM 87740
(505) 445-2847

Author's Page

Greg Satre was born in San Bernadino, California, in 1943. His father was lost in WWII, after which he lived in Colorado, Alaska, and Canada, where he spent several years on a wilderness ranch. In the years between the ages of three and nine, he was subjected to several near-death experiences which dramatically expanded his natural psychic talents and developed an ability to see the primary energy fields of biological life.

Greg returned to California in 1960 to live with his grandparents while completing high school. This circumstance was especially fortuitous, as his grandmother was able to guide him in organizing his burgeoning perceptual talents, drawing on a discretely held ancestral history of clairvoyant abilities. After high school, he pursued a formal education at San Diego State University for several years, with extensive studies in literature, philosophy, psychology, and art. The university resources also facilitated a personal endeavor to research the accumulated history of human mystical experience.

Following his academic studies, Greg married and welcomed a family of two children. While maintaining conventional employment for three years, he developed an independent means of livelihood as an artist, which he found harmonious with his continuing expansion and practice of metaphysical awareness. He developed an ability to do psychic readings and spiritual channeling with a focus on healing and positive life-choice resolution. The channeling brought recognition of reincarnational continuance and relevance to the current lives of many of the people with whom he shared the metaphysical arts. A profound transcendental experience at the age of 32 further expanded his understanding of multidimensional consciousness, spiritual value, and the gift of the opportunity of being in the multi-incarnational nature of human spirit and consciousness.

A friendship of singular and extra-ordinary dimensions was sparked when Greg met O.T. Bonnett at an art show in 1987. Together O.T. and Greg continue to explore the art and architecture of metaphysical consciousness as it applies to the everyday courses and potentials of human endeavor.

Greg is now living in Canon City, Colorado, in modest residence with two cats. His life continues to be inspired and sustained through loving conversation with his children Eric and Renee, and family and friends throughout North America and Australia.

Anyone wishing to correspond with Greg should send letters to the publisher and they will be forwarded to him.

Greg Satre
c/o Ozark Mountain Publishing, Inc.
PO Box 754
Huntsville, AR 72740

Other Books Published
by
Ozark Mountain Publishing, Inc.

Conversations With Nostradamus, Volume I....................by Dolores Cannon
Conversations With Nostradamus, Volume II..................by Dolores Cannon
Conversations With Nostradamus, Volume III.................by Dolores Cannon
Jesus and the Essenes.......................................by Dolores Cannon
They Walked With Jesus....................................by Dolores Cannon
Between Death and Life.....................................by Dolores Cannon
(Formerly titled Conversations With A Spirit)
A Soul Remembers Hiroshima.............................by Dolores Cannon
Keepers of the Garden.....................................by Dolores Cannon
The Legend of Starcrash...................................by Dolores Cannon
Legacy from the Stars......................................by Dolores Cannon
The Custodians...by Dolores Cannon
The Convoluted Universe, Book One.............................by Dolores Cannon
The Convoluted Universe, Book Two.............................by Dolores Cannon
Beauty and the Priest...................................by Reverend Patrick McNamara
I Have Lived Before......................................by Sture Lönnerstrand
The Forgotten Woman...by Arun & Sunanda Gandhi
Luck Doesn't Happen By Chance............................by Claire Doyle Beland
Mankind - Child of the Stars.......................by Max H. Flindt & Otto Binder
The Gnostic Papers...by John V. Panella
Past Life Memories As A Confederate Soldier...................by James H. Kent
Holiday in Heaven...by Aron Abrahamsen
Is Jehovah An E.T.?.......................................by Dorothy Leon
The Ultimate Dictionary of Dream Language.....................by Briceida Ryan
The Essenes - Children of the Light.........by Stuart Wilson & Joanna Prentis
Rebirth of the Oracle ....by Justine Alessi & M.E.McMillan

For more information about any of the above titles, soon to be released
titles, or other items in our catalog, write or visit our website:

OZARK
MOUNTAIN
PUBLISHING

PO Box 754
Huntsville, AR 72740

WWW.OZARKMT.COM
1-800-935-0045 / 1-800-230-0312 Wholesale Inquiries Welcome